THE SAS IN ACTION

SIDGWICK & JACKSON
LONDON

THE
SAS
IN ACTION

Peter Macdonald

First published in Great Britain in 1990
by Sidgwick & Jackson Limited

ISBN 0-283-06018-2

Printed in Great Britain by
Butler and Tanner, Frome, Somerset, for
Sidgwick & Jackson Limited
1 Tavistock Chambers, Bloomsbury Way
London WC1A 2SG

Editorial: Brown Packaging

Design: G. Bingham, S. Bleeze, D. Horwill and J. Tuttel

I would like to thank a number of former members of
the SAS, both regular and Territorial Army, who, for
reasons that are too obvious to mention, cannot be
named in this book. Some are still serving in other
corps or regiments, others have left the British Army
and returned to a more 'peaceful' life and I wish them
all the best of luck.

My thanks also to the many training establishments
that I have visited over the last few years: centres
where the Regiment trains and exercises, and whose
staff have given me an insight into the training. These
centres include No 1 PTS, RAF Brize Norton, ETAP
Pau, *Geb- und WiKmpf-Sch.*, Luttensee, and the
International LRRP School at Weingarten.

The writing of this book demanded much in the way of
research and I am indebted to Dr Terry White for his
contributions in this field to the chapters on Northern
Ireland and global counter-terrorist operations.

Editing the material submitted has been a laborious
task and I thank Chris Marshall for the thoroughly
professional job that he has done.

Front cover: Simulated hostage rescue. Siege-busting
is but one of the Regiment's roles.
Back cover: Armed with a Sterling sub-machine gun,
an SAS trooper on jungle patrol with Iban tracker.

CONTENTS

7 PREFACE

8 RAIDERS AND MISFITS

20 PROFESSIONAL WARRIORS

32 OUTPOSTS OF EMPIRE

44 LOOKING AFTER OUR FRIENDS

56 FIGHTING THE IRA

72 FIRE AGAINST FIRE

96 READY FOR ACTION

118 PREPARING FOR ARMAGEDDON

136 KEEPING UP TO SCRATCH

164 SPECIAL FORCES ON TRIAL

190 APPENDICES

PREFACE

In the poem-play *Hassan*, written by James Elroy Flecker, the Master of the Caravan questions a group of travellers thus,

> *'But who are ye, in rags and rotten shoes,*
> *You dirty-bearded, blocking up the way?'*

The reply, given by Ishak, the minstrel to the Caliph, is inscribed on the SAS memorial at Hereford,

> *'We are the Pilgrims, master; we shall go*
> *Always a little further: it may be*
> *Beyond that last blue mountain barred with snow*
> *Across that angry or that glimmering sea...'*

The information for this book has come from a multitude of sources. The book is not an official SAS Regimental history, for there is no such animal. Nor does it express the views, official or otherwise, of the Regiment, the British Army or indeed the British Government. *The SAS in Action* describes the operations and training of the SAS -- any views expressed are mine alone.

If this book is dedicated to any group of people, it is dedicated to the wives and families of the SAS Regiment, both regular and TA, who suffer loneliness and uncertainty, and without whom the men would not be able to do what they do best.

Simulated hostage-rescue. The lead man carries a Remington 870 pump-action shotgun.

RAIDERS AND MISFITS

The SAS owes its existence to a freak parachuting accident. Without this twist of fate, which gave David Stirling the chance to crystallise his plans for a crack commando force, one of the most famous units of all time might never have seen the light of day. But when it did, it seemed to have leaped from the pages of *Boy's Own*.

One day in July 1941, a tall, dark-haired man in the uniform of a junior officer in the Scots Guards approached the checkpoint outside Middle East Headquarters in Cairo. When stopped by the sentry he attempted to bluff his way through, but without success. Then, while the guard's attention was momentarily distracted by the arrival of a staff car, the subaltern slipped past and into the building. His disappearance did not go unnoticed by the sentry who realised that he had just been outmanoeuvred by a young lieutenant on crutches.

Once inside the headquarters building, the lieutenant entered the office of a major on the Adjutant-General's staff and identified himself. He said he needed to speak urgently with the Commander-in-Chief, General Sir Claude Auchinleck. The major was unimpressed. He recognised his visitor as an officer who had fallen asleep

An SAS trooper manning his twin Vickers K machine guns. The functional Arab headdress was adopted by a number of units in the Western Desert.

Above: This picture of David Stirling was taken shortly before his capture in 1943. He wears SAS insignia on his service-dress cap.

during one of his tactics lectures; he did not like him and refused to listen to his request. The telephone rang; it was the sentry reporting the intruder. While the major was otherwise engaged, the young officer slipped out of the office and into the corridor.

The next room he encountered was the office of the Deputy Chief of Staff, Major General Neil Ritchie. The lieutenant entered uninvited, apologised for his unconventional arrival and told the general he had matters of great operational importance to discuss. Impressed by the young man, despite, or perhaps because of, his daring approach, the senior officer invited him to sit down. The subaltern outlined his plan: to destroy Axis aircraft in the Western Desert whilst they were still on the ground. He would achieve this with a small team of hand-picked men who would parachute behind enemy lines before the next Allied offensive. General Ritchie listened attentively and with growing interest. The concept seemed sound and the young officer seemed convinced he could carry it off. The general approved the scheme and gave permission for the subaltern to raise his force. It would be known as L Detachment, Special Air Service Brigade. The name of the lieutenant, now promoted to captain and given charge of the new unit, was David Stirling.

Stirling was not a professional soldier but had joined up at the beginning of the war. At school and later at Cambridge, there was little to distinguish him from his contemporaries, apart, perhaps, from the fact that he stood six feet five inches tall. His major interest had been climbing; his ambition to conquer Everest. When war broke out, Stirling returned from the Canadian Rockies, where he had been training, and immediately joined the Scots Guards, a regiment with which he had a family connection. The following year he transferred to No 8 (Guards) Commando and at the beginning of 1941, sailed to the Middle East with 'Layforce', a combined force of three commando units, named after the founder of No 8 Commando, Brigadier Robert Laycock.

Stirling's 'chute caught and ripped on the plane's tail assembly

Layforce comprised a total of 2000 men. Its objective was originally the capture of the Greek island of Rhodes, but in February 1941, Rommel arrived in North Africa with the *Deutsches Afrika Korps* (DAK) and turned the tide of war against the British in the Western Desert. The Rhodes operation was scrapped and 'Layforce' was dispersed throughout the eastern Mediterranean theatre. No 8 Commando was based initially in Mersa Matruh, Egypt, from where it conducted a small number of unsuccessful commando operations against the Germans in Cyrenaica (the eastern portion of modern-day Libya).

Among the officers of No 8 Commando were a number of enterprising individuals, including J. S. 'Jock' Lewes, an Australian-born officer serving with the Welsh Guards. Together with his colleagues, including Stirling, Lewes began parachuting with some 'acquired' parachutes unloaded by mistake at Alexandria. If parachuting was in its infancy back home in Britain, it was non-existent in the desert. There were no instructors and no properly rigged aircraft, but, undeterred, Lewes and his fellow officers began training. Stirling was the first casualty. Jumping from a Valentia, an aircraft ill-designed for parachuting, Stirling's 'chute caught and ripped on the plane's tail assembly. He landed heavily on hard ground, severely damaging his back and suffering temporary paralysis of the legs. It was during the two months he subsequently spent in hospital that Stirling hatched the plan he presented to Major General Ritchie in July 1941.

L Detachment SAS Brigade began life at Kabrit in the Suez Canal Zone with three tents, a placard proclaiming

Right: Parachute training was in its infancy during the early days of the SAS. These troops are undergoing training on a flight-and-landing simulator somewhere in the Desert.

the new unit's identity, and a three-ton truck. There was of course no brigade, the title was used in attempt to convince enemy intelligence that there was a parachute formation at large in the Middle East. Nevertheless it was an independent command for the newly promoted captain (he reported directly to the Commander-in-Chief) and he immediately set about recruiting the six officers and 60 men he was allotted, drawing mainly on No 8 Commando. He soon raised his quota, but not without encountering some difficulty, as commanders were reluctant to lose good men.

Forced marches through the desert at any hour of the day were standard

From the beginning L Detachment attracted a high calibre of volunteers: experienced men who saw the chance to get to grips with the then rampant enemy. Stirling's first recruit was the parachuting Jock Lewes; the other officers were Bonnington, Fraser, McGonigal, Thomas, and Blair Mayne, a well-known Irish Rugby international who, at the time of his recruitment, was under close arrest for striking his commanding officer. Stirling also recruited soldiers and NCOs, among them Bennett, Cooper, Lilley, Rose and Seekings — names which would become synonymous with acts of daring and feats of endurance.

Now that he had the cadre of L Detachment, Stirling set about training them. Although many of the men had previously undergone commando training, they found Stirling's regime exceptionally hard. Forced marches through the desert at any hour of the day or night were standard; distances of 65km or more with weights of over 30kg were not uncommon. The ability to navigate was vital for all ranks and great emphasis was placed on endurance and willpower. Indeed, the early selection process of L Detachment bore a strong resemblance to that undertaken by prospective SAS members today. The skills and personal characteristics required have changed very little over the years.

Parachute training followed; the candidates practised jumping from scaffolding platforms, from grounded aircraft and off the back of moving trucks before graduating to the real thing. L Detachment had the use of a Bristol Bombay aircraft, a more suitable machine than the Vickers Valentia, but despite this advance two parachutists were killed on the first jump when their 'chutes failed to open. The problem was traced to the clip that connected the static line to the anchor rail inside the

aircraft. In certain conditions the clip could slip off the rail; without an anchor, the static line could not tauten and open the 'chute. A different clip was substituted and Stirling was the first to jump the following morning. His 'chute opened safely.

While training was in progress, Jock Lewes worked on developing a bomb which would be suitable for the type of operation L Detachment would be carrying out. Stirling's concept involved inserting small groups by parachute onto a Dropping Zone (DZ); from here they could move forward and attach explosives to enemy aircraft while they were on the ground. Therefore the explosive had to be light, as it had to be carried, but powerful enough to destroy an aircraft. After testing various mixtures, Lewes eventually came up with the combination of explosive, incendiary, oil, plastic and thermite which became known as the Lewes bomb.

L Detachment's first mission was timed to coincide with Operation Crusader, the offensive planned by General Auchinleck to begin on 18 November 1941. The enemy had a new type of ground-attack fighter — the Me 109F — based at the coastal airfields around Maleme and Tmimi. The plan was to drop the force onto two separate DZs from which it would launch its attacks on Tmimi, Maleme, and a third airfield at Gazala. L Detachment was to approach the airfields, lie low and observe during the day, then mount its attack the following evening — 17 November. The two parties were to move in under cover of darkness, plant their Lewes bombs on the aircraft, and move back inland to rendezvous (RV) with the Long Range Desert Group (LRDG). In the event, any chance the force may have had of accomplishing the mission was wrecked on landing.

One plane had to land after being hit by ground fire

On the evening of 16 November, despite severe weather conditions, 64 officers and men from L Detachment boarded five Bombays in Cyrenaica for the flight to the DZs. During the journey, the weather deteriorated still further: dense cloud obscured the DZs and the aircraft became lost. One plane, flying under the cloud in an attempt to get its bearings, had to land after being hit by ground fire; the remaining aircraft dropped their parachutists miles off course.

The situation was no better on the ground, however. Wind speeds at ground level averaged 70km/h, with gusts of up to 140km/h, and on landing the men were dragged off across the desert by their parachutes, some never to be seen again. Most of the supply containers were lost; those that were found contained some Lewes

Above: During a brief return to civilisation between operations, these troopers proudly display their hard-earned operational 'wings', worn on the left breast.

bombs but no fuses. Without these vital components the bombs were useless. The attack was called off, and in rain that turned the dried-up wadis into fast-flowing rivers, the survivors of the aborted mission made their way to the LRDG rendezvous. Out of the 64 that started out on the raid, only 22 survived.

One group walked onto the airfield before they realised where they were

Despite its disastrous start L Detachment was allowed to soldier on, and the men learned from their mistakes. It was obvious that the weather had played a decisive part in the failure of the operation by making accurate parachuting impossible. Parachuting could therefore not serve as the sole means of getting to a target area, and an alternative way of infiltrating behind enemy lines had to be found. The obvious choice was to adopt the LRDG approach and use vehicles.

The LRDG was equipped for its long-range reconnaissance role with stripped-down 30cwt trucks, modified for desert use and with a range of over 1600km without refuelling. Its commander, Major R.A. Bagnold, whose vehi-

cles had already ferried the SAS back from the failed Gazala raid, very graciously offered his unit's assistance in getting the SAS into target areas; Stirling gratefully accepted, realising that L Detachment could learn much from these veterans of desert travel.

Co-operation between the two units worked well from the start, and from their base at the Jalo oasis in the Libyan desert, patrols struck out at German airfields. Two operations were planned for 14 December. Sirte airfield, which lay to the west of Benghazi, would be attacked by troops led by Stirling and Mayne, while a force commanded by Lewes would strike at Agheila airfield situated between Benghazi and Sirte.

Escorted by S1 Patrol LRDG, Stirling and Mayne, together with 10 men, set off for Sirte, about 560km away. They travelled in seven 30cwt trucks, painted a dull pink to make them more difficult to spot from the air. The first 480km passed uneventfully; then, on the third day the convoy was spotted by an Italian reconnaissance plane.

The patrol's gunners engaged the aircraft, but it got away. The combined LRDG/SAS patrol then had just enough time to camouflage their vehicles in an area of scrub nearby before they found themselves being strafed by three Italian warplanes. Both men and transport escaped unscathed, but within six kilometres of the target they were again spotted and Stirling, reckoning that the enemy was now prepared for an attack, divided his force in two. One party, led by Mayne, would go on to raid the airfield at Tamit, about 50km to the west, while Stirling would lead the remaining men to Sirte on foot.

Stirling's group moved up to Sirte that night, walking right onto the airfield before they realised where they were. Escaping undetected, they moved to a ridge on the far side of the airfield. The plan had been to observe their target from this point throughout the following day and then move down during the evening and place charges

on the aircraft. But the following afternoon, Sirte was evacuated, leaving them no target to attack.

Mayne's team were more successful, destroying 24 aircraft with Mayne himself adding to his growing reputation. Having run out of bombs, he removed the instrument panel of one aircraft with his bare hands. The team also gate-crashed an aircrew mess party, engaging those present with smallarms at close quarters, and blew up the fuel dump.before they left. The raid lasted 15 minutes.

A raid led by Fraser resulted in the wrecking of 37 enemy planes

The airfield at Agheila, the target for Lewes's patrol, proved to be in use at that time only as a staging post and on the night of the SAS visit there were no aircraft on the ground. Not to be denied, Lewes switched his attention to a nearby house, which he understood was used as a conference centre by the enemy. Unfortunately the group's vehicles were identified as British before they got close enough to attack the building and Lewes and his men

Below: Keeping weapons clean was of primary importance in the Desert. The officer clears dust from the magazine housing of his Thompson, while the trooper loads a magazine.

came under heavy fire. Leaving half his force to return the fire, Lewes led the remainder to a nearby vehicle park where they placed 30 charges to good effect. In the resulting confusion, he and his men retired to safety.

The SAS had struck their first blows against the enemy, and were now, without a shadow of a doubt, operational. On 21 December one raid led by Bill Fraser on Agedabia airfield resulted in the wrecking of 37 enemy planes; two were left intact, causing Fraser to apologise for this 'failure'! By the end of 1941 the SAS had nearly 100 enemy aircraft to their credit — all destroyed on the ground — plus a number of vehicles and petrol stores.

They must have perished but for their bottomless reserves of cunning

But the detachment had also lost good men in the past two months, including Jock Lewes, gunned down by an Italian aircraft as his patrol were on the way back from a raid at Nofilia. It had also nearly lost a whole patrol. Returning from a fruitless attack on an airfield at 'Marble Arch', a group led by Fraser missed their RV and found themselves marooned in the desert over 300km from home. They had no option but to walk and must surely have perished but for their seemingly bottomless reserves of cunning and sheer nerve. When they were recovered over a week later, they had raided two enemy trucks, hijacked a German Army car and its crew, and rigged up a do-it-yourself water desalination plant into the bargain. This was by no means the only occasion on which SAS men were rewarded for their daring. In other cases individuals or even complete patrols disguised as Arabs or as Germans or Italians succeeded in deceiving the enemy.

A winged sword above a scroll bearing the motto 'Who Dares Wins'

Auchinleck's Operation Crusader had succeeded in driving Rommel back out of Cyrenaica and at the beginning of 1942 Tobruk and Benghazi were once again in Allied hands while the Axis forces were regrouping at Agheila. Stirling, mindful of the fact that Rommel was resupplied by sea, temporarily switched his sights from airfields to ports and presented Auchinleck with a plan for an attack on the harbour at Bouerat, a town on the Libyan coast, west of Sirte. The Commander-in-Chief, impressed by L Detachment's achievements, granted Stirling permission to recruit a further six officers and between 30 and 40

Right: David Stirling caught cat-napping against the wheel of a Willys jeep during a brief lull in operations. Rugged and manoeuvrable, the jeep was the ideal SAS vehicle.

men, and gave him access to No 8 Commando's recce unit, the Special Boat Section (SBS). A little later L Detachment was further reinforced by a Free French parachute squadron of some 50 'air commandos'.

Although the LRDG was still responsible for inserting L Detachment patrols, the SAS were quickly gaining experience and beginning to acquire their own identity. Until now each man had worn the badges and accoutrements of his parent unit, except on operations when the majority of SAS men sported Arab headdress in the manner of the LRDG. Nevertheless the SAS needed a trademark of their own and a new badge was designed, a winged sword above a scroll bearing the unit motto 'Who Dares Wins'. Popularly known as the 'winged dagger', the device is believed to represent either the flaming Sword of Damocles or Excalibur. The badge was first worn on a white beret, which was soon replaced by a sand-coloured

Left: Beards were common in the Desert, where water was at a premium. They were usually, but not always, dispensed with when their wearers returned to rear areas.

one. In addition to the cap badge, the SAS adopted their own parachutist brevet, comprising a parachute in the centre of the outstretched wing of the sacred ibis — a bird revered by the ancient Egyptians. A custom grew up surrounding the positioning of the 'Sabre' wings, as they became known. Newly parachute-qualified personnel wore them on the upper right arm, in the same position as the men of The Parachute Regiment and Airborne Forces wore theirs; once the wearer had distinguished himself on operations, however, the wings were transferred to the left breast. This tradition has been discontinued, although the wings themselves and the beret and badge are still in service.

The jeeps were fitted with twin Vickers K.303 machine guns

The SAS operation against Bouerat took place in late January 1942. A raiding force consisting of two SBS, 16 SAS and two RAF personnel was transported by the LRDG across the desert to the coast with the intention of attack-

ing enemy shipping. This time the operation did not go according to plan. The force had its transmissions picked up by German DF (Direction Finding) units, was harassed by Italian warplanes and lost its radio vehicle. Shorn of communications, it now had no idea what awaited in Bouerat. To make matters worse, one of the trucks now had a chance encounter with a pothole and the force's only canoe was damaged beyond repair. Unable to mine oil tankers in the harbour even had there been any (in the event there were not), the SAS party divided into two to assault secondary targets. One group, led by Stirling, located the petrol storage depot which it blew up, together with a number of petrol tankers and other supply vehi-

cles. The second group, under Captain Duncan of the SBS, destroyed the port's radio station. Both parties returned intact, despite the fact that Duncan's group ran into an ambush and had to fight its way clear.

As its experience and reputation grew the detachment became larger and better equipped. Although the LRDG was still relied on for many things, including its specialist knowledge and the training of navigators, L Detachment was developing towards its full potential. One area in which it was becoming increasingly independent was that of mobility. On a visit to Cairo in June 1942, Stirling managed to lay his hands on some 20 three-tonners; he also obtained an item of equipment which was to change the

face of SAS operations in the desert: the US-made Willys jeep. The SAS acquired 15 of these amazingly versatile four-wheel-drive vehicles and they were adapted to become agile, cross-country gun platforms. They were fitted with twin Vickers K.303 machine guns which in an earlier life had been mounted on RAF biplanes. Each vehicle carried two pairs — one in front of the navigator's seat and one in the rear of the vehicle — and certain SAS jeeps carried a Browning 0.5in machine gun, in addition to the Vickers and the crew's personal weapons. With their own jeeps and four-wheel-drive three-ton trucks, the SAS were now capable of transporting their own supplies and equipment. The new transport also allowed the

SAS to extend their operations and conduct patrols which lasted several weeks.

The start of SAS jeep-borne operations roughly coincided with the withdrawal of the Eighth Army to the defensive line of El Alamein as Rommel thrust his way back through Cyrenaica. The first patrols were carried out at the start of July 1942; the targets were the enemy airfields at Daba, Bagush, Matruh, Sollum and Fuka. On the raid at Bagush, charges were placed on the aircraft as usual, but only 22 of the 40 Lewes bombs exploded. Quickly rallying his men, Stirling led them across the airfield and shot up the remaining planes with eight Vickers, mounted variously on his staff car (the 'blitz-wagon'), a jeep and a three-tonner. The new technique worked well and Stirling wasted no time in trying it out again.

The next operation was against the Junkers Ju 52 airfield at Sidi Haneish, one of the Fuka aerodromes, and for this raid Stirling employed a fleet of 18 jeeps. Approaching in line abreast, the raiders were about a kilometre from the airfield when the runway lights were switched on for a returning aircraft. With the element of surprise still with them and the target well illuminated, Stirling opened up with his Vickers; the others quickly followed his example.

The whole area was clearly illuminated by scores of burning planes

On Stirling's command the patrol switched from line-abreast to arrowhead formation and the vehicles raced between rows of Heinkel, Junkers and Messerschmitt transport and combat aircraft. The runway landing lights had been switched off but the whole area was clearly illuminated by scores of, by now, burning planes. Stirling's vehicle was knocked out by enemy mortar and machine-gun fire, but, transferring to another, he led his patrol in a circuit of the airfield during which they destroyed further transport aircraft parked on the perimeter. The SAS then broke off the engagement and headed out into the desert. In two raids that evening L Detachment had destroyed between 40 and 50 aircraft, bringing its total 'kills' in the year since it was formed to around 250; a higher figure than that achieved by the RAF in the same period. L Detachment's achievement was not merely the destruction of enemy aircraft, which in itself contributed handsomely to the Allied effort, but to divert Axis troops from the front to guard the desert airfields. Auchinleck's faith in the SAS concept had paid off.

A *Luftwaffe* Me-109 fighter stands wrecked on the ground. During the campaign the SAS were responsible for destroying more aircraft than the Royal Air Force.

PROFESSIONAL WARRIORS

When Monty arrived in North Africa he was suspicious of the SAS; by the time he left, 'the Boy Stirling' and his men had succeeded in winning him round. But others in high places wondered whether the SAS were coming to the end of their usefulness. Born in the desert, the SAS seemed destined to die in the desert, the victims of their own success.

In the struggle to eject the Axis from North Africa, the SAS established themselves as a force to be reckoned with, continuing their raids on airfields and harassing the enemy in support of Monty's push west. Nevertheless, they were still not universally accepted by the more orthodox soldiery and when victory was finally achieved in the desert in May 1943 and the Allies turned their attention to Sicily and Italy, the fate of the SAS seemed to be in the balance. In the end there was a role for them, but not before they had undergone considerable reorganisation.

By the start of 1943, the Special Air Service had come a long way from their small beginnings at Kabrit. In October 1942, the month in which the battle of Alamein began, L Detachment had been accorded regimental status as the 1st Special Air Service Regiment (1 SAS) and with the addition of the remaining elements of No 8 Commando and the SBS and volunteers from the Greek 'Sacred Squadron', the SAS continued to expand. With a second regiment (2 SAS), to be commanded by his brother William, in the pipeline, Stirling, now a lieutenant colonel, was well on the way to realising his current vision of three SAS regiments, one for each operational theatre. But no sooner had these forces come together than his own capture at the beginning of 1943 by a German counter-insurgency patrol (he was subsequently

Captain McDonald, SAS, meeting with local partisans during operations in northern Italy.

21

incarcerated in the maximum-security prisoner-of-war camp at Colditz) took him out of circulation at a critical time. This combined with the end of the desert campaign thwarted his plan for a full-scale SAS brigade. Indeed as operations closed in North Africa, the SAS became fragmented: the French SAS Squadron detached itself from the British Army and joined the Free French, laying down the foundations for the future 3 and 4 SAS; the 'Sacred Squadron' returned to Greek control. Stirling's old command, 1 SAS, was seemingly earmarked for disbandment but was reprieved. A and B Squadrons were renamed the Special Raiding Squadron (SRS) with Major Paddy Mayne, Stirling's natural successor, in command. Mayne was promoted lieutenant colonel and took the 250 officers and men of the SRS to Palestine for training. At the same time D Squadron SAS, a unit of similar strength under the command of Earl Jellicoe, also went to train in Palestine and became the Special Boat Squadron. Up to this time, Special Boat teams had been part of the SAS; this reorganisation signalled the parting of the ways. Meanwhile 2 SAS moved to Algeria where it began recruitment and training.

In one action alone the SRS captured three coastal batteries

The landings in Sicily went ahead in July 1943 and the Special Air Service were involved in tackling a number of targets in advance of the main force. In one action alone the SRS captured three coastal batteries, killing over 100 enemy and taking a further 600 prisoner — all at a cost of only one man dead and six wounded. But these were tactical, rather than strategic, operations, more suited to commando or parachute units than the SAS. What is more, during the preceding months, the Special Raiding Squadron had been training in Palestine and the Lebanon for mountain and ski warfare with a view to possible deployment in the Balkans. Despite the fact that elements of 2 SAS parachuted into the north of Sicily during the 38-day campaign, the SAS were generally deployed out of role — not the first, nor the last, time they would be misused in this fashion.

Dudgeon was captured and murdered after a contact with Germans

Although David Stirling's capture had proved a great blow to the SAS (his powerful personality had dominated and controlled the organisation he had created), his loss was not as catastrophic as some have suggested. The SAS continued to evolve, with Bill Stirling originating many new and successful concepts. At his suggestion 2 SAS

Above: A signaller taps out a message on his morse key. Signalling skills continue to play a vital role in SAS operations and all patrols have a communications specialist.

Above: SAS officers attending a combined-arms briefing. Careful planning and preparation lie behind the Regiment's many successes.

became heavily involved in the strategic battle for Italy which followed the Italian capitulation in September 1943. Operations in the Western Desert had proved that the SAS were at their most effective when operating behind enemy lines. Therefore when the Allies moved to drive the Germans from the Italian mainland, the SAS were once again sent to cause havoc at the enemy's rear.

One SAS operation which began right at the start of the Italian campaign was Operation Speedwell. The aim of 'Speedwell' was to destroy railway lines between Genoa and Spezia; Bologna, Pistoia and Prato; and the line from Florence to Arezzo. Two SAS parties were parachuted in. One, under the the command of Captain Pinckney, dropped to the south of Bologna; the second, led by Captain Dudgeon, was to destroy the lines between La Spezia and Genoa. The operation began on 7 September 1943 and both patrols had mixed fortunes. Pinckney was lost on landing, but two of his teams destroyed a total of four trains. One of Dudgeon's teams

succeeded in wrecking a further two trains, although Dudgeon himself, together with an SAS trooper called Brunt, was captured and murdered after a contact with Germans; two NCOs who went missing are believed to have met the same fate.

'These men are very dangerous...they must be ruthlessly exterminated'

The murder of captured SAS men was in accordance with a personal directive issued by Hitler. In it he stated that 'captured special forces troops must be handed over at once to the nearest Gestapo unit...these men are very dangerous, and the presence of special forces troops in any area must be immediately reported...they must be ruthlessly exterminated.' The directive, initially issued because of SAS successes in the Western Desert, had not been implemented by Rommel. In Italy the situation was very different and SAS officers and men, once caught by the enemy, could expect only torture and death. Nevertheless, the tragic losses apart, Operation Speedwell was a success. The two SAS patrols had succeeded in hampering the movement of German reinforcements to

southern Italy at a time when they were urgently needed, although whether Allied planners took advantage of the situation is open to debate.

Other operations in which the SAS took part during September 1943 included a landing by the SRS at Bagnara on the toe of Italy and a pathfinder operation carried out by 2 SAS at Taranto for the 1st Airborne Division; in October both units were involved in the successful battle for the Adriatic port of Termoli. But by this point SAS involvement in Italy was drawing to a close, at least for a time. After deploying small groups to attack German lines of communication and recover POWs released after the Italian capitulation, the SAS retired to Britain for reorganisation before the D-Day landings.

HQ SAS Troops came under the direction of 'Boy' Browning

In January 1944 the SAS Brigade was formed under the command of Brigadier Roderick (later General Sir Roderick) McLeod. Comprising the SRS (now once again under the title of 1 SAS), 2 SAS, the 2nd and 3rd Free French Parachute Battalions (later 3 and 4 SAS), the Belgian Independent Parachute Squadron (later 5 SAS), and F Squadron GHQ Reconnaissance Regiment (Phantom), the brigade had a strength of around 2500 all ranks. HQ SAS Troops came under the direction of Lieutenant General Frederick 'Boy' Browning, commander of the 1st Airborne Division, and a liaison section was created within the division to co-ordinate SAS activities.

Dropped into occupied territory, recce teams contacted the resistance

Heading the liaison staff was Lieutenant Colonel I.G. Collins, an experienced special-operations planner who was responsible for liaising between the SAS and other groups, including the SOE (Special Operations Executive). He had a difficult task, for although by this time the majority of British military commanders had realised that special forces such as the SAS and SBS had an important role to play in modern warfare and original misgivings about the relative values of 'private armies' had been shelved by all but the most obstinate, few people understood the effective use of SAS troops. A number of suggestions for their possible employment bordered on the suicidal. In fact the proposed misuse of the SAS in a purely tactical capacity in the Normandy invasion

Early 'hearts and minds'. Deprived of both creature comforts and family life for long periods, troopers take the opportunity to comfort a small child.

Two NCOs, probably SBS, defusing mines in Greece. While the SAS operated in Italy and Northwest Europe, The SBS wrought havoc in Italy and the Eastern Mediterranean.

prompted Bill Stirling to resign as commanding officer of 2 SAS. He was replaced by Lieutenant Colonel Brian Franks and the role of the SAS in the battle for Northwest Europe was eventually worked out.

Although they were not directly involved in the D-Day landings, the SAS did get to go to war in France and Belgium in a strategic role. They were under the control of the 21st Army Group for operations around the Loire, Paris and Abbeville and were directed by Supreme Headquarters Allied Expeditionary Force (SHAEF) for operations in Belgium and the remainder of France. Dropped into occupied territory, reconnaissance teams contacted local resistance organisations and evaluated the general situation. If an area seemed ripe for exploitation, reinforcements were brought in and a base established.

Once in position, the SAS advised, and on occasion trained, the local resistance fighters; they also conducted their own guerrilla war against the occupying forces, usually within a radius of up to 80km from each base. Bridges were blown, railways destroyed, trains derailed and roads mined. Enemy convoys were attacked and bases targeted for RAF bombing missions.

The RAF (38 Group, 46 Group and the Special Duty Squadron) were responsible for the insertion and resupply of the SAS operating in France and Belgium. Although the role was a new one for them they carried it out with great skill, often overcoming difficulties imposed by the lack of effective communications. Besides the normal supplies of arms, ammunition and explosives, the RAF brought in jeeps. These vehicles, similar to the ones used in North Africa but without the desert adaptations, were partially fitted with armour plate. They were to prove of great value to the SAS and a real menace to the Germans.

On occasion SAS vehicles travelled unidentified within German convoys

One of the SAS missions launched in support of the Allied invasion of Northwest Europe was Operation Houndsworth. Inserted into eastern France just before D-Day, the SAS, with the help of a three-man team of guides (a so-called 'Jedburgh' team), set up a base from which they carried out a series of successful attacks over a three-month period. Apart from earmarking targets for the RAF, this group, which eventually comprised around a squadron of SAS officers and men, blew up the Dijon, Lyons and Paris railway lines a total of 22 times, caused over 200 enemy casualties, and took over 100 prisoners.

A similar operation conducted over a two-month period during the summer of 1944 was Operation Gain. A party of around 60 men, this time of D Squadron 1 SAS, was tasked with, among other things, disabling the railway system in the area of Rambouillet, Orleans and Chartres. This jeep-borne squadron, commanded by Major Ian Fenwick, operated with great flair, and nowhere is this better illustrated than in their methods of attacking German supply convoys. Finding that the enemy moved at night with lights on, Fenwick ordered his detachments to do the same, and on occasion SAS vehicles actually travelled unidentified within German convoys. By the time they withdrew to Allied lines towards the end of August, Fenwick's party had scored a number of notable victories at a cost of 10 men. One of these casualties was Fenwick himself, who was killed trying to crash through a German ambush. 'Gain', like 'Houndsworth', made an impact out of all proportion to the size of the force involved and caused severe disruption within the enemy's rear echelon.

Apart from these operations carried out from established bases, the SAS were also sent in to conduct a series of assaults on specific targets in the enemy rear areas in the lead-up to the invasion. Thus on D-Day minus one, 18 SAS teams were dropped into France to attack enemy lines of communication in support of the Allied advance from the bridgeheads. As the invasion progressed and the Allies broke out from the Normandy beaches and began to push inland, the SAS were ordered into northern France. A series of operations was conducted during this phase of the advance, including Operation Loyton, under the command of Lieutenant Colonel Franks.

The aim of 'Loyton' was to locate suitable targets for the Allied air forces, at that time enjoying air superiority, and generally to harass the enemy with a view to preventing free passage of reinforcements to the front line. After gleaning as much information as possible from SOE and MI6, Franks sent in a reconnaissance party under Captain Henry Druce. However, on his arrival Druce was disturbed by the attitude of the Maquis with whom he was supposed to liaise in organising the DZ for Franks and the main party. Ten days afterwards his fears about the reliability of the local resistance group were confirmed when one of their number turned informer.

The confusion only ceased when Druce shot the suspect dead

The result of this treachery was the seizure of the Maquis' radio. Druce had been forced to rely on the resistance for communications because his own wireless set had been damaged during the drop; he now found himself without access to a radio. Nevertheless he found other means of getting his message through and managed to bring in the remainder of the SAS group, but as Franks and his men dropped onto the DZ on the night of 31 August/1 September, smallarms fire suddenly broke out on the ground. Apparently, one of the Maquis, already suspected of being a traitor, had opened up with a sub-machine gun (SMG) while attempting to escape. Other resistance fighters opened fire in the confusion which only ceased when Druce shot the suspect dead.

With the arrival of Franks and his group, Operation Loyton got under way. The SAS commander had only 87 men at his disposal as he preferred to avoid contact with the unreliable local resistance wherever possible. This small force executed a number of successful actions and were responsible for the diversion of two German divisions from the front. Tasked solely with eliminating the SAS, these troops were prevented from joining the battle and were instead forced to roam the countryside hunting an elusive enemy.

But these victories were not achieved without loss. When the survivors of 'Loyton' exfiltrated through to the

A 3in mortar crew in action, somewhere in northern Italy. When the SAS finally left the peninsula, the war in Italy had only a fortnight to run.

Allied lines between 9 October and 12 October, more than 30 men were missing. Of these, 28 were known to have been captured alive and were subsequently tortured and killed by the Gestapo. After the war it was discovered that these men had gone to their deaths bravely and a number of their murderers were apprehended and brought to justice, but at the time it was a high price for the SAS to pay despite the success of the operation. SAS activity throughout France continued in a similar vein until the end of 1944 when the Allies reached the borders of Germany. At this point, 3 Squadron 2 SAS, commanded by Major Roy Farran was despatched to Italy to fight alongside the partisans.

The squadron arrived in Italy in December 1944 and their area of operations was the north of the country. Although untried, 3 Squadron was highly trained and rar-

ing to go. Volunteers were continually being selected, many with a wealth of previous experience in other fields of warfare and eager to prove themselves within the SAS. Farran himself was a career officer but he was as capable of the unorthodox as the most flamboyant wartime volunteer. Indeed when the unit began Operation Tombola in March 1945, the squadron commander, ordered by 15th Army Group not to accompany his unit, contrived to 'fall' from one of the Dakotas while despatching his men. It was no accident.

Farran ordered a howitzer, interpreters — and a Scottish piper

'Tombola' was conducted in the area between Spezia and Bologna — the same area in which Pinckney and Dudgeon had operated the previous year. The aim of the operation was to train Italian partisans and direct their activities against German occupying forces in the Tuscan Apennines. Up until this time guerrilla operations in the

Loaded down with ammunition, the crew of a Vickers heavy machine gun pass through a small Italian town, following in the wake of the German retreat.

area had been co-ordinated by SOE under the command of Captain Mike Lees. The guerrillas themselves were a mixed group comprising Italians and Russians, communists and republicans, deserters and escaped prisoners of war. On his arrival, Farran inspected these men, some of whom were still in their early teens, and decided that something drastic would need to be done to turn them into a fighting force. He immediately submitted a long list of supplies, including a 75mm howitzer, interpreters in Italian, Russian and German, khaki berets with coloured hackles — and a Scottish piper. The latter, along with the berets, was intended to inspire the Italians. These sup-

plies plus arms and ammunition were dropped in shortly afterwards and training began. Within a fortnight Farran's guerrilla battalion was ready for its first operation.

The SAS and partisans carried out an attack on the HQ of LI Corps

The area of operations for 'Tombola' was bordered to the north by the River Secchia and close to Mount Cusna; it was highly suitable for guerrilla warfare. Farran's force based itself in a remote valley high in the mountains where they used the 75mm howitzer as the basis for a defensive position known as the Cisa Box. Towards the end of March, the squadron put into action an idea originally conceived by Captain Lees when they carried out an attack on the headquarters of the German LI Corps at

Villa Rossi. The Germans occupying the building put up heavy resistance and despite all attempts by the partisans remained in control of the upper floors. Meanwhile an assault on the Villa Calvi, timed to coincide with the Villa Rossi assault, was more successful.

The assault party inadvertently crossed a minefield

Nevertheless the assault party lost the element of surprise early on in the operation. As they attempted to gain entry to the Villa Calvi, after inadvertently crossing a minefield, but without mishap, they encountered and were forced to engage a four-man German patrol, alerting the Germans inside the building who opened fire. However, the attackers still managed to break in and kill the occupants of the

In the final stages of the war, the SAS deployed an increasing number of jeep patrols to attack enemy lines of communication in their rear areas.

ground floor, among them Oberst Lemelson, the German chief of staff. Under cover of Bren-gun fire laid down by men outside the villa, the partisans set fire to the house and made good their escape, heading in the opposite direction to the way they had come and away from their hide-out in the mountains to a rendezvous with the remainder of the 'Tombola' base group.

The link-up was achieved after 20 hours of marching over rough country and a night crossing of the River Secchia. The attackers progress was initially slowed by two men who had been wounded by a grenade during the final assault and the party's leader, an SAS officer

Above: A tour of the docks. Special Air Service units were in at the death of the campaign in Northwest Europe and were among the first units to reach the Baltic.

named Harvey, called for volunteers to take care of the most severely wounded man. Two men remained with the casualty and nursed him back to the hide-out while the rest withdrew to the RV at a quicker pace. Here they lay up for a few hours to recover from their ordeal before setting off to the Cisa Box shortly after daybreak.

The partisans first action had been a considerable success, despite the fact that a signal had been sent by 15th Army Group to prevent it going ahead. Farran, aware of the adverse effect that a last-minute cancellation would have on morale, conveniently managed to 'have left' before the message arrived. Estimated enemy casualties of the operation were around 60, including a large number of German officers, while Farran's group lost three killed and 14 wounded or missing.

The Germans were constantly harassed by the SAS and partisans

There followed a number of actions around the River Secchia, while the Germans made repeated attempts to track the guerrillas down. The SAS sent out fighting patrols, usually half British and half partisan in make-up, and a number of pitched battles took place in which the Anglo-Italian force usually emerged the victors despite the enemy's numerical superiority. The fortunes of war were rapidly turning against the Germans and they were dispirited. The advancing American 1st Armoured Division began to push the remaining three German divisions back across the River Secchia and towards the Po. All the time they were constantly harassed by the combined SAS and partisan force. By the time Farran received orders to exfiltrate his squadron, the war in Italy had only a fortnight to run.

While 3 Squadron 2 SAS was on operations in the Tuscan Apennines, the remainder of the SAS Brigade had been busy conducting reconnaissance missions for the British and Canadian armies advancing into Germany. In April 1945, with the end of the war in sight, the SAS were active in Holland, Belgium and Norway. They were in at the kill in Northwest Europe, but ironically the demise of the *Wehrmacht*, once the world's most effective war machine, heralded their own disbandment — for a time at least.

Right: Mopping-up operations. The SAS were employed rounding up suspected war criminals. Here a jeep patrol escorts Gestapo agents back for interrogation.

OUTPOSTS OF EMPIRE

The SAS did not survive the end of World War II and went the way of the other 'private armies'. Many of its soldiers had been wartime enlistments and those of them who had survived the conflict now returned to civilian life, while the career men and the volunteers who stayed on in the Army after the war moved to other units. But the SAS was not a passing fad. The Stirling concept lived on in the minds of all those who had served with the unit and they remained convinced that the Army needed the SAS. The nature of post-war conflict was to prove them right.

The SAS Brigade, like so many wartime special operations forces, was disbanded in 1945; only one small unit remained and that was 'semi-official'. In the post-war chaos that followed the Allied victory in Europe, a six-man team began investigations into the murder of captured colleagues. A mass grave had been discovered at Gaggenau, near Baden-Baden, which contained the bodies of some of the 28 SAS men captured on Operation Loyton. The War Office was making no effort to investigate the disappearance of SAS

Returning from operations in the jungle, an SAS patrol waits for the next train down the line. The SAS, as the Malayan Scouts then as 22 SAS, spent nine years on operations in Malaya.

men on active service, and there was no concerted effort to bring German service personnel to justice for carrying out Hitler's infamous 'Commando Order'. This prompted Lieutenant Colonel Brian Franks to pursue the murderers himself.

There were a number of reasons for this seeming apathy on the part of Allied governments. One was the political embarrassment caused by the fact that the Vatican was linked with a major Nazi escape line. The second was that both British and American intelligence organisations were recruiting former SD and SS officers for operations in Eastern Europe. Concerned that the perpetrators would escape, Franks set up his own investigations unit under the command of Major Eric Barkworth, who, together with Company Sergeant Major (CSM) 'Dusty' Rhodes and four others, continued the chase after 2 SAS was disbanded. Reporting back through the Phantom signals set-up to HQ SAS, the team was responsible for the capture of a number of Gestapo officers involved in the murder of captured SAS personnel and SOE agents — all this despite attempts to prevent it operating in the British sector of occupied Europe.

A squadron from 21 SAS was on its way to the Malayan Emergency

Although the British SAS ceased to exist with the end of World War II, abroad the situation was very different. The French and Belgian SAS units became established in their respective countries' armed forces. France's 3 and 4 SAS became *2e* and *3e Regiments Chasseurs Parachutistes* (RCP); the latter still retains the SAS Sabre wings as the predominant feature of its unit emblem with below it the words 'Who Dares Wins' in English. Meanwhile the 1st Battalion Belgian Para-Commandos retained the 'winged dagger' as its cap badge, and continues to maintain the traditions of 5 SAS. Nevertheless within two years of the war's end there was once again a British unit wearing the insignia of the SAS — albeit not a regular one.

In 1947 a Territorial Army — that is, a volunteer — unit known as the 21st Special Air Service Regiment (Artists' Rifles) was formed with none other than Lieutenant Colonel Brian Franks as its first commanding officer. The Artists' Rifles was a London-based TA unit originally raised in 1860 and known for providing 'officer material' for other arms and corps in wartime. This 'marriage' between the SAS and such a unit was to prove productive: the formation of 21 SAS (Artists) reintroduced a

Malayan Scouts in the early days of jungle warfare in Malaya. Members of a four-man patrol pose before setting off into the rainforest.

J.M. 'Mad Mike' Calvert, exponent of long-range jungle patrols and founder of the Malayan Scouts, one of the foundations of 22 SAS.

number of former wartime SAS officers and men back into the military system. Four years later a squadron from 21 SAS was on its way to take part in the Malayan Emergency — the conflict which was to bring about the rebirth of the SAS as a full-time British Army regiment.

Chin Peng conducted a campaign of violence against the authorities

Since 1948 ethnic Chinese communist terrorists (CTs) had been engaged in a campaign of terror in the rural areas of Malaya; they were experts at jungle warfare. One of the communist leaders was Chin Peng, who had been awarded the MBE for his services to the Crown during the Japanese occupation of Malaya. Together with a number of his former comrades from the SOE-sponsored Force 136, Chin Peng conducted a campaign of violence against the authorities. With arms, ammunition and explosives supplied by the Allies during the war and afterwards secreted away in jungle caches, the CTs were adept at striking vulnerable targets before disappearing back into the impenetrable jungle. To combat this, in 1950 the British raised a counter-insurgency unit — the Malayan Scouts — which specialised in extended jungle patrols and locating and ambushing the elusive CTs. The unit was commanded by its creator, Major J. M. 'Mad Mike' Calvert a jungle warfare veteran of the Burma campaign who had commanded the SAS Brigade in Europe towards the end of the war.

Calvert started recruiting his force of jungle fighters locally from British forces stationed in the Far East. One of the problems he faced was that his somewhat easy-going unit did not always attract the right sort of volunteer. While many, including a number of National Servicemen, were skilled soldiers, there were some who chose the Scouts as a way of avoiding the discipline of more conventional areas of the Army. It took some time before this 'undesirable' element could be 'weeded out' and they were to colour military opinion against the Malayan Scouts, and subsequently against the SAS, for some time to come. But Calvert was aided in his task of selecting more suitable volunteers by Major John Woodhouse, who went on to create an SAS selection programme which remains the basis for the one now in use.

Calvert was forced to deploy his troops with the minimum of training

The 100 men raised in the Far East became A Squadron Malayan Scouts (SAS). Two further squadrons were recruited from totally different sources. B Squadron, which arrived in Malaya in 1951, was drawn wholly from the ranks of 21 SAS and included many wartime veterans (although they had no experience of jungle operations they had the 'flexible approach' so often associated with the SAS and were eager to learn); C Squadron, on the other hand, was the result of a recruiting drive carried out by Calvert in Rhodesia.

One of the major problems faced by all the squadrons was the lack of qualified instructors and the lack of adequate training in jungle warfare techniques. The jungle with its inherent dangers and diseases, was a difficult place to survive, let alone conduct successful counter-insurgency operations. Yet under pressure from senior military commanders Calvert was forced to deploy his troops with the minimum of training. The Rhodesian squadron for example, had only three weeks of jungle training before being set to work, and this was given by Woodhouse and an NCO with less than a year's in-theatre experience between them.

Despite the early problems of indiscipline, and the fact that training was primarily conducted while on operations, the Malayan Scouts (SAS), renamed the 22nd Special Air Service Regiment (22 SAS) in 1951, achieved a number of successes. They proved the viability of extended jungle operations at a time when it was generally considered that Europeans were incapable of surviving the hostile environment for long periods. One patrol spent a total of 103 consecutive days on operations, its only contact with the outside world during this period being aerial resupply and radio communications.

A rapport had to be built up between the aboriginals and the Regiment

The central pillar of British policy in Malaya was the 'Briggs Plan', a campaign to win the 'hearts and minds' of the local population. The CTs faithfully followed Chairman Mao Tse-Tung's philosophy of using the peasant population as a source of food, shelter, and potential recruits. The plan, named after the Director of Operations in Malaya, General Sir Harold Briggs, was designed to prevent this idea of guerrillas moving among peasants like 'fish in a sea' from working. Thousands of locals were relocated in safe villages (*kampongs*): with the 'sea' drying up, the 'fish' would be forced to head for deeper water; that is, retreat further into the jungle.

By 1952 22 SAS was on the offensive. The CTs, lacking the support of the local population, withdrew still further into the jungle. Once totalling more than 10,000 men, the terrorist army had dwindled to less than 5000, and the CTs were forced to operate in small bands for fear of detection. The Regiment itself began to develop a unit identity during the campaign but also underwent a number of changes. Mike Calvert was invalided out in 1951 and was replaced by Lieutenant Colonel John Sloane, a more orthodox soldier who introduced more traditional military discipline to the SAS. In 1953 Oliver Brooke took over and did much to further the growing relationship between the Regiment and the Malayan aboriginals. When Brooke was seriously injured during a parachute descent his place was taken for a short period by Mike Osborne who, in turn, was replaced by George Lea. Lea had much to do with shaping the SAS, in particular building up a strong cadre of officers.

A number of squadron commanders also left their mark on the Regiment, among them John Edwardes, Harry Thompson, Peter de la Billière and John Woodhouse. Indeed it was the latter who suggested employing aboriginal tribesmen in the war against the CTs. Before the aboriginals could be expected to co-operate, however, a rapport had to built up between them and the Regiment. The way in which this was achieved became almost a blueprint for later SAS 'hearts and minds' campaigns.

To begin with, a number of jungle forts were established by the Regiment. Attracted by free food, medical treatment and protection from the CTs, local tribesmen would trickle into the forts and set up their 'bashas' next

Aerial resupply was vital for patrols operating deep in the jungle. The success of many SAS operations depended on the support of the RAF and Royal Army Service Corps.

to those built by the SAS. Eventually these jungle forts became permanent, defended encampments — a safe haven for the local tribes for miles around. Once a fort had been established, its running would be handed over to the police or Malayan security forces and the SAS would go and build another. In this way a chain of forts was constructed down the centre of the country, effectively controlling the area and denying it to the terrorists.

Doctors and RAMC NCOs held sick parades for the natives

The medical help played an important part in building confidence between the troopers and the tribesmen, many of whom were suffering from easily cured diseases. Doctors and Royal Army Medical Corps (RAMC) NCOs attached to the SAS held sick parades for the natives; the RAF dropped medical supplies and, on occasion, arranged a helicopter ride for the local headman, thus demonstrating both British strength and a genuine interest in the welfare of the local population. The 'hearts and

minds' policy paid off, and the aboriginals responded by passing on information on the whereabouts and movements of CT groups. In this way the 'eyes and ears' of the security forces were extended into the most inaccessible areas of the 'ulu', as the jungle was known.

Navigation over the hilly terrain had initially proved almost impossible

Woodhouse returned to Britain in 1953 and set about developing a standard selection programme. A number of new faces were recruited into the Regiment, and a number of familiar ones returned. Men who had served with the LRDG and the wartime SAS volunteered, and some of them were to have a marked influence on the SAS in years to come. One such officer was Dare Newell, a former SAS officer with experience in guerrilla warfare gleaned from wartime operations in Albania and Japanese-occupied Malaya. Dare Newell went on to become Regimental Adjutant, while Woodhouse eventually took command of the Regiment.

The SAS, first as the Malayan Scouts and then as 22 SAS, spent a total of nine years on operations in the Malayan jungle out of a campaign which lasted 11 years in all. During this period the SAS perfected the techniques and tactics demanded by jungle operations and, from the experience, learned a great deal which would stand them in good stead in the campaigns to follow. Navigation over the often hilly terrain, in hot and humid conditions, had initially proved almost impossible. However the SAS perfected the use of the prismatic compass, a skill which had to be mastered by all volunteers who sought to gain entry to the Regiment. In addition much was also learnt about the art of jungle survival. Living in primitive conditions the SAS troopers acquired new skills from the aboriginals and from Iban trackers brought to Malaya from Sarawak. They learnt preventative medicine from the RAMC medics, signalling from attached signallers, and a host of other technical skills associated with patrol operations.

Once snagged the parachutists lowered themselves by means of a rope

One such technique perfected by the SAS during their time in Malaya was parachuting into primary jungle — a highly dangerous activity. SAS men were dropped into the jungle canopy with the expectation that their 'chutes would become caught up in the trees as they fell. Once securely snagged the parachutists lowered themselves to the jungle floor by means of a rope. This method could be employed only in primary jungle, where there was sufficient strong foliage to support a man long enough for him to make his way down to earth under his own steam.

Jungle DZs were only used on operations. They were located and marked out by Auster pilots (the Auster was a light observation aircraft flown by the Army Air Corps) and a number of successful airborne insertions were conducted during the Malayan campaign. In 1953 a total of 177 men from the three squadrons were dropped into the jungle for Operation Termite, with only four minor casualties.

55 Company lost over 100 men killed when planes crashed into the jungle

Using this method of insertion patrols were able to extend their area of operations further than conventional troops. Food and other supplies proved a limiting factor initially, but the Regiment devised and introduced a special 7-14 day SAS patrol ration, allowing men to operate for up to two weeks without resupply. Nevertheless patrols relied heavily on air support for insertion, resupply and casualty evacuation.

Aerial resupply was not always easy as is evident by the casualties incurred by 55 Company Royal Army Service Corps (RASC). Responsible for despatching supply containers to the ground forces from RAF aircraft, 55

Above: Elephants were just one means of transport tried out in the difficlult terrain of Malaya. The elephant experiment proved unsuccessful, however!

Company lost over 100 men killed when planes crashed into the jungle. As helicopters were scarcely out of their infancy, fixed-wing aircraft had to be used, including Hastings, Valettas and, towards the latter stages of the campaign, Beverley transports. Stores and equipment were parachuted down onto the jungle canopy and collected by troops on the ground. However, as helicopters became capable of carrying a greater payload and operating at higher altitude, the reliance on fixed-wing aircraft lessened. Towards the end of the conflict both Royal Navy and RAF helicopters were used increasingly and a number of injured SAS soldiers owe their lives to the skill and dedication of the pilots.

The structure and organisation of the SAS evolved and became established during the Regiment's time in Malaya.

Right: Rivers, although they did not take as direct a route as an elephant could, proved far more reliable as a means of inserting and extracting patrols.

The original three squadrons (A, B and C) that had formed the Malayan Scouts had been augmented by a fourth (D Squadron) before Calvert left for the UK. Then in 1956 a further squadron, the Parachute Regiment Squadron, was raised from volunteers drawn from the Paras and commanded by Major Dudley Coventry. That same year C Squadron returned to Rhodesia to become the Rhodesian SAS and was replaced by a New Zealand squadron under Major Frank Rennie. This Kiwi connection meant that a number of Fijians joined the Regiment. These men were excellent soldiers and many were to spend their entire service life with 22 SAS.

When propaganda failed, the CTS resorted to terror

By 1958, the year in which 22 SAS became established in the British Army ORBAT (ORder of BATtle), the war in Malaya had turned in favour of the security forces. The communist groups became more fragmented, many of their leaders being killed or captured. Food was scarce outside the forts and protected *kampong*s and recruits were difficult to come by. When propaganda failed, the CTs resorted to terror.

One of the last of the communist leaders to be rounded up was Ah Hoi, also known as the 'baby killer', after the gruesome disembowelling of an informer's pregnant wife. Local villagers had been forced to watch this atrocity as Ah Hoi tried to prevent further co-operation with the security forces. After the killing Ah Hoi took his small band further into the jungle and sought shelter in the Telok Anson swamp, to the southwest of Ipoh. The British administration, determined to kill or capture him, selected the SAS to go in after him and his men.

D Squadron's initial task on landing was to create a Landing Zone

In February 1958 D Squadron HQ and three troops, 37 men in all, parachuted into the swamp, about five kilometres from its western edge. During the descent into the heavily forested area, one soldier, Trooper Mulcahy, severely injured his back when his canopy collapsed as it hit the tree tops. D Squadron's initial task on landing therefore was to clear a number of trees to create a helicopter Landing Zone (LZ) from which Mulcahy could be 'casevaced'. In an impressive display of flying the pilot brought the helicopter into the small clearing and hov-

A Special Air Service patrol carrying out final equipment checks before boarding the aircraft that will drop them deep in the Malayan jungle.

ered just above the swampy ground while the casualty was loaded aboard.

After the successful evacuation of the casualty the squadron fanned out to search for CTs. Various deserted camps were found but the enemy managed to evade the SAS until a young aboriginal with one of the patrols spotted a couple of terrorists on the bank of the Tengi River. Two members of the patrol, Sergeant Sandilands and Corporal Finn, crossed the river behind a log, opening fire on the two terrorists when they came within range. One was killed outright but the second, a woman, made off at speed and was soon lost in the dense jungle. Following up the track made by the fleeing woman, the troop found a recently deserted camp. The CTs were on the run, and D Squadron responded by placing a cordon around the area. Two days later a small, emaciated woman came out of the jungle to negotiate surrender terms. The terms put forward by the the female CT, whose name was Ah Niet, included a general amnesty for all jailed communists and a large sum of money for the

A wounded communist terrorist, captured during a contact with a patrol, is held under guard before being moved to a rear area for interrogation by Special Branch.

CT team. These unrealistic terms were immediately rejected and Ah Niet was released to inform Ah Hoi that he either brought his band out, or the RAF would conduct a bombing raid on his hiding place. Faced with this choice, Ah Hoi and the remnants of his group gave themselves up over the next 48 hours.

The SAS had won from Whitehall the right to exist as a regiment

Morale among the communists was at an all-time low. Before his surrender Ah Hoi had been forced to move his hiding place 18 times over a period of three months, because of aggressive patrolling by the security forces. In addition he had lost two of his men in contacts with SAS patrols. Other CT bands were in a similar position and over the next few weeks further terrorists surrendered, sometimes alone but occasionally in groups. The Malayan Emergency was drawing to a close.

The 22nd SAS Regiment left Malaya with three major achievements under its belt. First it had proved that European troops could operate in a hostile environment for months, when previously the maximum duration for an infantry patrol was considered to be seven days. As a

A trooper kitted out for tree-jumping, an effective but dangerous method of inserting patrols into the remote areas in which the communists were operating.

result of these patrols, the security forces had been provided with intelligence, considered by many to be more important than the 108 confirmed CT kills in nine years. Secondly, the SAS had proved the value of the 'hearts and minds' concept in modern COIN (COunter-INsurgency) operations and had lived for long periods with the natives, winning them over to the administration's cause and gaining valuable allies. These lessons were used to advantage by the SAS in their later campaigns in Borneo and Oman, and in Southeast Asia by their American Special Forces counterparts. Finally the SAS had won from Whitehall the right to exist as a regiment. This was a victory well deserved and perhaps the greatest single achievement of their campaign in Malaya.

43

LOOKING AFTER OUR FRIENDS

The SAS left Malaya as past-masters in counter-insurgency. This had not gone unnoticed in higher circles, and over the next two decades whenever Britain needed to help a threatened friendly government, the SAS were the first to get the call. In most cases full-blown British intervention was out of the question and the SAS plus the locals were able to sort things out.

The SAS Regiment's performance in Malaya ensured that it survived the reorganisation of the British Army in the late 1950s. Nevertheless sacrifices had to be made and 22 SAS was reduced in size to two operational squadrons — A and D. It was already in this streamlined state when an emergency arose in late 1958. That November, D Squadron departed the Far East, bound for the Middle East and war in an environment as different from the jungle of Malaya as it was possible to be.

A member of a four-man patrol providing medical aid to a Dyak in a remote area of Borneo. The Regiment's 'hearts and minds' campaign was a great success.

During the 1950s, anti-government guerrillas under Talib ibn Ali, began a long and bloody struggle for control of Muscat and Oman (the Sultanate of Oman since 1970) on the Arabian Gulf. Although the Sultanate was a backward country and its people were poor, it dominated the Straits of Hormuz, the major sea route for oil leaving the Gulf for the open Arabian Sea. For this reason, it was a traditional ally of Britain, so when the Sultan could no longer cope, it was to Britain that he went for help.

The climax to the campaign was in true SAS style

By 1957 the rebels had been driven back by a joint British-Omani force to Jebel Akhdar, a mountainous area rising to 8000ft and surrounded by a fertile plain; it was a seemingly impregnable stronghold. The British decided to use airpower to try and dislodge the insurgents, but this failed, and a conventional infantry assault against such a target was deemed out of the question. There was nothing for it but to send for the SAS, who arrived at the end of 1958. Even for the Regiment it was not all plain sailing and D Squadron — the first to arrive — took losses as it adjusted to the terrain, the weather and the new enemy. But a quick result was wanted before the campaigning season ended and so in the New Year A Squadron arrived as reinforcement and the final assault on the mountain was planned.

The climax to the campaign took place at the end of January 1959 and was in true SAS style. Diversionary attacks were made to disguise the main assault which took the form of an amazing ascent up onto the plateau at the base of Aqbat Dhafar, the rebel stronghold. The SAS men took a seemingly unclimbable route and their arrival at the top took the insurgents by surprise; in fact the rebel machine-gunners were not even manning their weapon on that side, so safe did they feel. The 'impregnable' Jebel Akhdar was taken and victory soon followed.

On its return from Oman, the Regiment passed through a period of operational inactivity. Advantage was taken of the lull to brush up individual and troop skills. Troopers were sent on outside training courses, exercises were conducted overseas and in 1960 22 SAS moved its HQ from Malvern to Hereford where it established itself at Bradbury Lines. It was almost four years before the SAS received their next operational assignment.

In December 1962 there was an internal rebellion in Brunei, a British protectorate, which, together with Sarawak and Sabah, formed the northernmost third of Borneo, an island to the east of Malaya; the remaining two-thirds of the island belonged to the independent state of Indonesia. The 'Brunei Revolt', as the localised

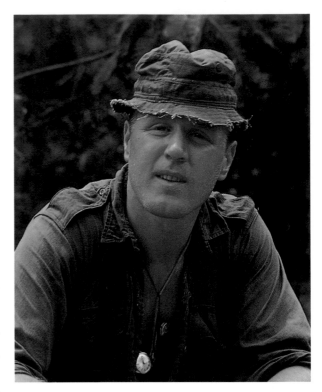

Above: Sunlight was not a problem in the deep, dark recesses of the jungles of Borneo and this trooper has adapted his bush hat accordingly.

rebellion was known, was organised and led by a young Brunei sheikh named Azahari, who wanted to unite the three dependencies. It was short-lived but dramatic. Small parties of armed guerrillas simultaneously attacked a number of strategic targets, including police stations, government buildings and a power station. Britain responded quickly. Troops stationed in Singapore, including Gurkhas, Royal Marine Commandos and soldiers of the Queen's Own Highlanders, were rapidly deployed to Brunei to suppress the revolt. Eight days later the rebellion was over and the 1000 or so guerrillas who had taken part had disappeared into the jungle.

Nevertheless the situation on the island of Borneo was still unstable. An expansionist Indonesia under President Sukarno was seeking to acquire further territory in the region and regarded the rest of the island of Borneo with covetous eyes. It was into this scenario, with Indonesian-backed guerrillas poised just the other side of the 1100km

Right: Carrying an Armalite, a trooper moves along an aerial walkway. The local population were adept at building such structures over the many gorges in the operational area.

frontier, that A Squadron 22 SAS, at its own request, was propelled in January 1963.

At that time the Director of Operations in Brunei was Major General Walter Walker, an officer who appreciated the value of the SAS and was pleased to have their assistance. Walker had five infantry battalions under his command and they, together with a single SAS squadron, were expected to secure the far-reaching frontier, an apparently impossible task. The terrain was varied and difficult: primary and secondary jungle, hills and mountains, swamps and fast-flowing rivers. The latter were the main arteries of communication in the thick impenetrable jungle. Along them, in longhouses built on stilts, lived the majority of the local population. Walker realised that the Regiment had experience in conducting long-range patrols and so he immediately deployed A Squadron into the jungle. He reckoned that the skills learned in Malaya, the SAS' familiarity with the 'ulu', and their ability to co-operate with local natives, would provide him with a vital asset in the coming struggle. He was right.

Shortly after its arrival A Squadron fielded a total of 21 patrols along the frontier. Although the border with Indonesia was ill-defined the SAS had two distinct advantages over the rebels when it came to locating crossing-points and mounting ambushes. Firstly, because of the

Above: A patrol test-fires its weapons before going out into the jungle. The American Armalite rifle was generally preferred to the SLR by members of the SAS.

nature of the terrain there were only a limited number of crossing-points and the SAS were professional soldiers, better at concealing their whereabouts than partially trained guerrillas. Secondly, the local tribes could probably be persuaded to provide them with advance notice of enemy movement. During its time in Malaya the SAS had come close to perfecting the 'hearts and minds' technique and they set about employing it again during the Borneo 'Confrontation'.

One NCO manufactured an improvised hydro-electric generator

After keeping a village under observation, to establish where its allegiance lay, a patrol would pay a visit to the headman. Depending on how friendly the village was, they would either sit around and talk or, if things went well, eat and drink with the villagers. Once initial contact had been made, they would then withdraw to their jungle hide-out, and lie up for anything up to a week before returning to pick up where they had left off.

Visits to the villages were never hurried affairs and the SAS never forced themselves on the natives. Before long the visits became longer, perhaps with a patrol spending first one night, then another in 'their' particular village. In this way a relationship was established and soon there were a number of patrols operating out of the villages. The tribespeople provided food and accommodation, trackers if the village was in the jungle, transport and guides if it was on a river. The SAS in return brought gifts, provided medical care for the sick, and in some cases carried out building work. Unknown talent began to emerge. One NCO, 'Gypsy' Smith, manufactured an improvised hydro-electric generator but is perhaps better known in Regimental folklore for his alcohol still. Smith is reputed to have made the still using the frame of a bergen rucksack, but the exact details of its design remain a secret to this day.

Through this and other means a bond of mutual respect and admiration was forged between the natives and the troopers. The tribesmen supplied the patrols with information which they in turn passed on to their brigade HQ. One tribe, the Iban, had supplied trackers for the SAS in Malaya; old acquaintances were renewed and a number returned to work for the Regiment.

The Ibans 'were state of the art at tracking and trapping'

An old Borneo hand describes Iban proficiency:
'They were state of the art at tracking and trapping. On one occasion their skill even boggled my mind. We were moving towards an enemy force and the (Iban) tracker, who had been following the tracks of three or four people all morning, returned and said "One of the patrol is an officer and he is wearing brown boots, carrying a pistol, has an assault rifle, a bush hat..." I said, "Hold on, wait. I mean I know you're very good at tracking and I know that you're much better at reading signs than we are but how, in the name of Christ, do you know what sort of hat he's got on, what sort of weapons he's carrying?" And the tracker said, "Oh, he's over there." And through a thin screen of trees there was a clearing in which stood an [Indonesian regular army] officer.'

At the end of April, D Squadron replaced A Squadron and spent much of its tour training locally raised scouts together with the Gurkha Independent Parachute Company. Although there was no common language the Border Scouts learnt quickly and became both efficient

Below: Weapons and belt-kit on board, the troopers prepare to launch their native canoe into a fast-flowing river. The river could be dangerous: boats were vulnerable to ambush.

A signaller sending his message while watched by the remainder of his patrol. Native longhouses were often given over to SAS patrols by the Dyaks.

and effective. The SAS were greatly helped in their training of the locals by attached specialists, including linguists from other units.

The rebellion in Brunei ended in 1963 and the war then began

The Regiment had its first casualties of the campaign in May 1963 when a helicopter crashed in bad weather. Among the nine people on board were: Major Norman MBE, MC, second-in-command of 22 SAS and, like Dare Newell, a veteran of the guerrilla war against the Japanese; Major Harry Thompson MC, the man behind the capture of Ah Hoi in the Telok Anson swamp; and Thompson's signaller Corporal 'Spud' Murphy. Aircraft crashes caused almost as many casualties as did contacts with the Indonesians, and this loss was a particular blow to the Regiment. Thompson had been due to take over command of 22 SAS the following year.

Tension along the border with Indonesia was increasing and more casualties were to follow. A United Nations team visited Borneo during 1963 to assess the feelings of the local population. That summer the Federation of Malaya accepted Sarawak and Sabah into what then became the Federation of Malaysia, while the Sultanate of Brunei chose to remain a British protectorate. As the politicians made their plans the Indonesians acted and in August 1963 launched a major cross-border offensive.

According to General Walker, the rebellion in Brunei ended in 1963 and the war then began.

A helicopter descends into a Landing Zone prepared by the SAS. Helicopters provided invaluable support throughout the Borneo Confrontation.

'You could actually hear this zone of silence move towards you'

Indonesia's first major incursion into Borneo came just as D Squadron was leaving and A Squadron was returning for its second tour. As the conflict escalated the decision was taken to re-form B Squadron and training was underway by December. The following October B Squadron was manned and ready, and supported by a cadre of NCOs from A and D Squadrons it deployed to Brunei for the first time. Despite the additional manpower the Regiment was fully stretched. To ease the pressure, it was augmented by the Guards Independent Parachute

Company, a unit of the Household Division, which was later to become G Squadron 22nd SAS Regiment, and SAS selection courses were run in-country.

By the end of 1964 there were 18 British infantry battalions on active service in Borneo, a total which included eight Gurkha battalions. In addition there were three Malaysian Army battalions bringing the number of troops deployed to 14,000, including supporting arms and services. Most of these men were deployed in the jungle and some were better suited to operations in this strange environment than others. A former SAS NCO, who now runs a survival school, explains:

'A lot of soldiers from other units found the jungle in Borneo very disturbing, and some soldiers in regular infantry units actually died of shock. This is one of the reasons, apart from the type of action fought in Borneo, why the Gurkhas, Paras, Marines and SAS were involved so heavily.'

The sergeant goes on to describe his first experience of the jungle and the effect it had on him:

'I was very keen to see the jungle and the animals and the birds, so psychologically I was looking forward to it. However, nothing prepared me for the first few steps through the foliage. It was like leaving a room with a 1000-watt bulb and entering a room with a 20-watt bulb. It was dark and gloomy. Instead of seeing the animals and being surrounded by them, as they sensed you coming and heard the sound, they would move off. So you were immediately surrounded by a zone of silence instead. Often, when you made contact with the enemy, it would be because you weren't moving at a time when he was moving past you. You could actually hear this zone of silence move towards you, or move parallel to you, more than you could hear the enemy patrol.'

In the late summer of 1964 the SAS established a number of training camps for Border Scouts in northern

Armed with an L42 sniper's rifle and carrying a light anti-tank weapon across his bergen, a trooper keeps watch for the *adoo* in Oman in the early 1970s.

Borneo and western Sarawak. From among those trained the SAS selected 40 Iban Dyaks for cross-border operations. The Iban were just one of the Dyak tribes living in Borneo; there were also Land Dyaks, Muruts and Punans — all with their own customs and way of life. Until fairly recently some of these tribes had been headhunters (some still were according to some sources) and most were deadly accurate with blowpipes which could fire a poison dart up to 50m. The Dyaks were a very introverted people and given to killing trespassers, rather than warning them off. A number of Indonesian soldiers who strayed into Dyak territory did not live to regret their intrusion. It paid to have them on your side.

Hit in the left thigh, Thomson was flung to one side

The situation in Borneo continued to hot up and the SAS were authorised to patrol up to 25km into Indonesia. These operations were codenamed 'Claret' and a brief summary of one such cross-border patrol gives an idea of what these missions could be like, and an insight into the make-up of the SAS soldier.

In February 1965 a patrol was approaching what appeared to be a long-vacated guerrilla camp when the lead scout, Trooper Thomson, saw an Indonesian soldier just as the latter opened fire. Hit in the left thigh, Thomson was flung to one side and landed in a clump of

bamboo, next to a second Indonesian whom he promptly shot dead. Meanwhile the patrol commander, Sergeant Lillico, returned fire despite also having been hit in the initial burst. The remainder of the patrol immediately dispersed and laid down a barrage of fire. The Indonesians, perhaps under the impression that reinforcements had been brought up, apparently withdrew. Lillico, himself unable to walk but believing Thomson capable of doing so, ordered the lead scout back to bring forward the remainder of the patrol. Thomson crawled onto a nearby ridge, put down some fire in the direction of the guerrilla camp and, after applying a tourniquet and shell dressing to his shattered leg and taking a dose of morphia, continued his crawl towards the patrol's ERV (Emergency RendezVous). The remainder of the patrol meanwhile had decided to withdraw to a nearby infantry position to raise a force to return and sweep the contact area.

The sergeant was now alone in the jungle. He dragged himself into the shelter of a clump of bamboo, bandaged his wounds and injected himself with morphia. He then passed out and remained unconscious until awoken by a helicopter hovering over the jungle canopy. Lillico reckoned that he must be invisible among the bamboo and so resolved to crawl to the ridge, where the foliage was less dense, the following morning.

By late the following afternoon, as Thomson was being recovered by the follow-up patrol having dragged himself 1000m, Lillico had reached the ridge as planned.

He fired a few shots to attract the attention of the search party he knew would be out looking for him, but his attempts to signal for help were answered by bursts of automatic fire from close by and he was forced to remain silent while the Indonesians carried out a search of the area.

Lillico had to watch as a friendly helicopter came and went

The enemy failed to find him, but his position was now overlooked by an Indonesian soldier up a tree 40m away. This meant that Lillico could not signal to his would-be rescuers and he had to watch as a friendly helicopter came and went. Fortunately just before last light the helicopter returned; this time the sergeant managed to attract the crew's attention and was winched to safety. For his part Sergeant Lillico was awarded the Military Medal and Trooper Thomson received a Mention in Despatches.

In the summer of 1965 the British battalions in Borneo were reinforced by the arrival of Australian and New Zealand forces from the 28th Commonwealth Brigade, Malaysia. These included two SAS squadrons — one from New Zealand and one from Australia. Activity in the bor-

The terrain in Oman was varied but *jebels* such as this were typical features. From the high ground, a small party of men could hold up an entire company or more.

The rugged terrain of South Arabia was familiar to the SAS in the 1950s, 1960s and 1970s. This trooper keeps watch with a 7.62mm Light Machine Gun (LMG).

der areas increased and patrols often faced large groups of Indonesian regulars, often paratroopers or marines. Reconnaissance and ambush patrols were sent out to cover rivers and trails used by the Indonesians, enemy bases were attacked and the SAS acted as guides for larger infantry formations. The Regiment remained closely involved in the conflict, with its squadrons serving four to five month tours on rotation.

At the start of the 1970s the Regiment was once again back in Oman

Singapore opted out of the Federation of Malaysia in August 1965 and two months later there was an appallingly violent coup in Indonesia. After some months of bloodletting during which there were an estimated 600,000 deaths, Sukarno, the Indonesian leader, was replaced by General Suharto. A peace agreement was signed in August the following year, and the 'Confrontation' came to an end. It had been one of the least publicised campaigns since World War II, lasting

four years and costing the lives of 114 British and Commonwealth soldiers. Of these, three were from 22 SAS, which also lost two men wounded in the nine operational tours it completed during the conflict. Borneo had been difficult, but it had also been successful, and the SAS had played an important part in the victory.

At the start of the 1970s the Regiment was once again back in Oman. Sultan Qaboos was fighting overthrow by rebels in Dhofar, a region of Oman which bordered the Marxist People's Democratic Republic of the Yemen (PDRY), to which the rebels could turn for aid and shelter. Qaboos turned to Britain for support and it was decided to send in the SAS, who were not only trained in counter-insurgency operations but also capable of providing medical aid to the Dhofaris. It was hoped that the SAS 'hearts and minds' approach developed in Malaya and Borneo might succeed where other methods had failed. The first squadron arrived in February 1971, and until September 1976 the Regiment maintained at least one squadron in Oman on a four-month operational tour.

The SAS troops which deployed to Dhofar were split into groups known as BATTs (British Army Training Teams). These raised and trained units of varying size called *firqat* units, which contained local men, many of whom were former guerrillas (*adoo*). The SAS also established CATs (Civil Action Teams), comprising a medic, a vet and at least one Arabic speaker. Both BATTs and CATs did much to win over the local Dhofaris.

However, following a series of successful SAS/*firqat* operations between March and October 1971, the *adoo* decided to strike back and on the night of 18 July 1972 250 *adoo* attacked the town of Mirbat. Supported by heavy machine guns, mortars, 75mm recoilless rifles and one Carl Gustav anti-tank weapon, the *adoo* were fortunately spotted by a patrol of the Dhofari Gendarmerie and the element of surprise was lost as the sound of smallarms fire alerted the eight SAS soldiers within the perimeter. Their commander, Captain Kealy, immediately made his way up to the roof of the 'BATThouse', as the SAS quarters were known, to assess the situation.

The defenders' only heavy weapon was an ancient 25-pounder field gun

About 100m to the northwest was a small fort defended by some 30 *askars* (armed militia from northern Oman). These, together with about 25 gendarmes holding a larger fort 700m to the northeast, were now returning the *adoo* fire. Instantly, on the 'BATThouse' roof, Corporal Chapman and Lance Corporal Wignall took up position behind a 0.5in Browning machine gun and a General Purpose Machine Gun (GPMG), while Lance Corporal Harris set up a mortar at the foot of the building. Nevertheless the defenders were outnumbered and outgunned; their only heavy weapon was an ancient 25-pounder field gun at the Gendarmerie Fort. Acting purely on instinct, a Fijian, Trooper Labalaba, raced across to the gun pit to assist the Omani gunner.

Kealy had only recently joined the Regiment and, at 23 years old, was relatively inexperienced. He nonetheless quickly realised that the key to Mirbat's defence was the Gendarmerie Fort and the gun. If the guerrillas were denied this position, there was a chance that the defenders could hold out until air support could be called in. Informed by his radio operator, Savesaki, that Labalaba had been wounded, Kealy agreed to the former's request that he be allowed to go over to the gun pit. The second Fijian covered the 700m to the fort under heavy enemy fire and, by some miracle, made it unscathed.

Concentrating their fire on the fort and 25-pounder position, the *adoo* stepped up their attack and some guerrillas managed to break through the camp perimeter despite the accurate fire being laid down by Chapman and Wignall on the BATThouse roof. The situation was becoming increasingly desperate. Kealy got on the long-wave set and radioed for an airstrike and helicopter casevac. Then, unable to reach the gun pit on the shortwave,

Kealy, together with an SAS medic named Tobin, raced across to the Gendarmerie Fort, leaving Corporal Bradshaw to direct fire from the BATThouse.

In the gun pit both Fijians were badly wounded but were still firing at the enemy closing in on their position. Captain Kealy and Savesaki engaged the advancing *adoo* at close quarters with smallarms and grenades, while Labalaba continued to operate the 25-pounder until he fell. The Fijian was quickly replaced by Trooper Tobin, who managed to fire one more round before he himself was fatally wounded.

Strikemaster jets arrived and, directed by Bradshaw, engaged the guerrillas

Kealy radioed Bradshaw, telling him to aim the mortar rounds closer to the gun pit and was informed that the air support was on its way. Soon after, Strikemaster jets arrived and, directed by Bradshaw, engaged the guerrillas with cannon, driving them back with heavy casualties. Further sorties were directed against the rebels heavy weapons on Jebel Ali while a relief force comprising members of G Squadron 22 SAS and led by the squadron commander, was brought in by helicopter. These 23 men, who had been training at Salalah when the attack began, carried nine GPMGs between them. They were landed to the southeast of the BATThouse and fought their way to the SAS at the gun pit. The battle for Mirbat was over.

The successful defence of Mirbat against a well-equipped, brave and determined enemy was in many ways the turning point of the campaign. Although Kealy's detachment lost two men dead and two more were seriously injured, the guerrillas lost over 30 men and many more later died of their wounds. But more important than the figures is the fact that this victory did much to rob the *adoo* of their influence over the Dhofaris — influence which increasingly accrued to the SAS and the *firqat*.

In his book, *SAS: Operation Oman*, General Tony Jeapes, an SAS squadron commander in Oman, describes how the success of the *firqat* led to the eventual victory. The Regiment must take much of the credit for this success for it remained the backbone of the *firqat* despite the fact that there were often less than 50 and rarely more than 100 SAS personnel deployed to Dhofar at any one time. In 1974, the Sultan had 15,000 troops deployed fighting the *adoo*; a year later these forces were augmented by 1600 men from 21 separate *firqat* units, all trained and administered by the SAS.

The campaign did not end until 1975, by which time the *adoo* had lost their support both inside and outside Oman. In the five years of fighting, the Regiment had lost just 12 men killed, including the two who died at Mirbat.

FIGHTING THE IRA

What the SAS role actually is in Northern Ireland has, over the years, given rise to much speculation and controversy. Yet the Regiment's primary function in what is Britain's longest-running conflict this century, is intelligence-gathering. Despite the often tedious nature of this work, it can be no less dangerous than direct confrontation, and its results, in terms of hard information, are invaluable to the Security Forces.

From the covert observation post (OP), it was possible to detect almost any movement in the surrounding fields and along the narrow tarmacadam road that reached across the border. The border itself seemed more imaginary than real — there was nothing obvious to indicate the divide between Northern Ireland and the Irish Republic. The local civilian population on both sides of the border knew exactly where it was, as did the men that manned the OP. The difference was, the locals could cross it with impunity.

Inside their camouflaged hide, which was totally concealed from the outside world and formed part of a natural hedgerow, four men lay in cramped conditions. Two of them were resting in the two green sleeping bags. The third maintained a radio watch on the set strapped to the top of his bergen, while the fourth scanned the surrounding countryside slowly through a pair of high-power, fixed-focus binoculars, while making occasional entries in a brown, plastic-backed notebook.

Armed with an SA 80, a member of a foot patrol stops a vehicle in an area near the border with Eire. Temporary checkpoints deprive terrorists of freedom of movement.

Ready to move at a moment's notice should their position be compromised, the men spent their time in alternate states of bored lethargy or slumber, and constant alertness. At pre-set intervals, the 'watchers' rotated with the 'sleepers' in a system known as 'hot-bedding', squirming into the warm, recently vacated sleeping bags as the others took over the observation duties.

The SAS in Ulster wage an unrelenting war against an experienced foe

The patrol manning the OP had been in position now for three nights and two days, and would remain there until they either saw what they had come to see, or were recalled or replaced by another team. All four men belonged to an SAS squadron deployed to Northern Ireland as part of the British Army's counter-terrorist campaign in the Province.

Although not unaware of the policies and politics involved in the conflict, the men maintained a 'professional' detachment from everything but the job in hand. Above all, they were experienced, extensively trained professional soldiers, not the 'hit squad' that their enemies, mindful of their many successes, tried to maintain they were.

SAS counter-terrorist and intelligence-gathering operations in the Province usually, but not always, pass unnoticed by all but the most ardent speculators. Unseen by enemies and friends alike, the SAS in Ulster wage an unrelenting war against an experienced foe. It is a war that, for the British Army as a whole, has dragged on since 1969 when troops were deployed to Northern Ireland as the latest round of sectarian troubles broke out.

Troops were sent to the Province in 1969 to protect the Catholic community from violence at the hands of the more prosperous and powerful Protestant population. Faced with the task of maintaining law and order it was inevitably not long before the Army succeeded in alienating both sides. The Catholics turned to the Irish Republican Army (IRA), but the latter were without weapons and experienced men. Further, there was a split occurring in the ranks between those who held to the IRA's socialist ideology (the line of what was to become the Official IRA) and those who favoured direct action. The result was that a new organisation emerged — the Provisional IRA (PIRA), the 'Provos' — and went to war on the Protestant paramilitaries, and eventually against the British Army. In the early period stones and petrol

An extremely high standard of fieldcraft is required by patrols operating in the border area. Camouflage and concealment are vital SAS skills.

bombs were the main weapons used against the soldiers, but in the end these gave way to firearms and in February 1971 a British soldier was killed — the first since the 1969 deployment. In the ensuing months, the violence turned from rioting to terrorism: innocent civilians on both sides of the sectarian divide were picked up and murdered in gangster-style executions, bombs exploded in shops and public houses, and off-duty soldiers were targeted for assassination. On the one side were the Protestant Orange paramilitaries; on the other nationalist republicans. The latter were particularly strong in Belfast and Londonderry and in the border areas of Tyrone, Fermanagh and Armagh; the southern section of the last mentioned — South Armagh — was the major stronghold in what became known as 'Bandit Country'.

The British Government responded to the escalating violence by adopting the techniques that had proved successful in counter-insurgency operations in Malaya and Kenya. Intelligence units were formed to take the war to the terrorists. They were given the task of capturing IRA men and turning them back on the enemy as informers.

The document instructed the wounded to lie still and pretend to be dead

On 22 June 1972, one such unit came to light when soldiers in civilian clothes opened fire with a Thompson sub-machine gun within the republican Andersonstown district of Belfast. Four civilians, including a republican politician, were wounded. One of the soldiers, charged with attempted murder, identified his unit as the Mobile Reconnaissance Force (MRF). The soldier was acquitted, and an angry Northern Ireland Civil Rights Association (CRA) claimed that this had been but one of many such attacks on non-military republicans, and they issued a pamphlet advising the public 'What to do if the SAS/MRF shoot you'. Among other things, the document instructed the wounded to lie still and pretend to be dead until the squad left. The Civil Rights Movement — and some journalists — believed that the MRF were waging a 'Phoenix-style' assassination programme; that is, similar to that operated by the Central Intelligence Agency (CIA) in Vietnam. The aim, it was suggested, was to eradicate the republican political infrastructure.

The SAS, however, was not even in the Province in 1972, and so was unable either to operate on its own or to serve with the MRF. Elements of D Squadron had been sent to the Province for several weeks in 1969, during which time they maintained an unusually high profile; they even laid a wreath on the grave of Lieutenant Colonel 'Paddy' Mayne at Newtownards cemetery. In addition, senior SAS officers were undoubtedly rotated

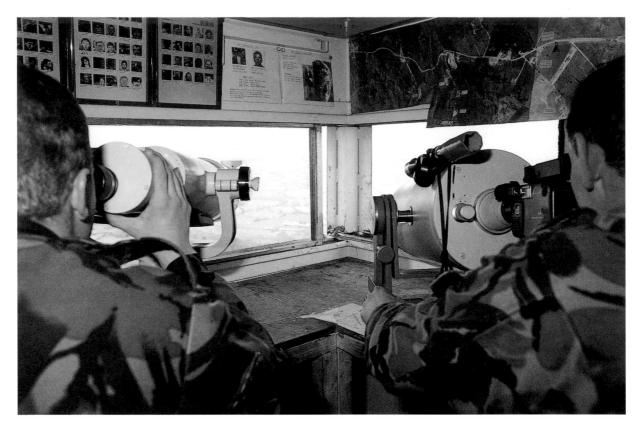

Manning an overt OP, these soldiers scan the surrounding countryside for any sign of unusual activity. Surveillance, both and open and covert, provides constant intelligence.

through intelligence posts in the Province during the early 1970s, although some of them had already completed their tour of duty with the Regiment and had returned to their parent units by the time of the republican allegations. In fact it took a series of grotesque acts of terrorism before British Prime Minister Harold Wilson took the controversial step of ordering the Regiment into the Province in 1976.

On 4 January five Catholics were killed in two shooting incidents

After a bloody 1974, talks between representatives of the Foreign Office and the IRA in January 1975 resulted in a temporary halt to hostilities between the latter and Army. But sectarian violence continued and indeed some of the most appalling episodes of the 'Troubles' took place during this year. One of the most notorious incidents occurred on 1 August, when Orange paramilitaries, wearing the uniform of the Ulster Defence Regiment (UDR),

murdered three members of the popular Irish group, the Miami Showband. The IRA later responded by bombing a Belfast bar and killing five people. Altogether 1975 turned out even worse than the previous year, for although the actual number of terrorist attacks went down, the number of deaths from sectarian violence rose from 216 in 1974 to 247 in 1975. The IRA were assessed as being responsible for 60 per cent of these deaths.

The ceasefire with the Army came to an end in November 1975 and at the start of 1976 came the series of events that precipitated the arrival of the SAS in the Province. On 4 January five Catholics were killed in two separate shooting incidents. The following day six IRA men stopped a bus in South Armagh. After releasing the Catholic driver, they machine-gunned the Protestant passengers: 10 were killed, only one survived. Two days later, a squadron of the SAS was deployed to the Province, with 11 soldiers being immediately despatched as the squadron's advance party. Within a year, a second squadron followed, together with signals support. The initial brief of the SAS was to destroy the PIRA leadership in South Armagh. Never again were the gunmen to feel safe in Bandit Country, where the kill ratio had formerly been fifty-to-one in favour of the terrorists.

The fields and hedgerows of South Armagh were a far cry from the jungles of Southeast Asia and the deserts of the Middle East. For a start, the population of the area was not obviously susceptible to a 'hearts-and-minds' approach. However, there were similarities: the border — marked by lane, hedgerow and stream — was easily crossed, particularly at night, and the isolated farmhouses on the Eire side of the border provided a sanctuary from the British Security Forces. An SAS sergeant describes how operations were carried out in early 1976:

'Our four-man patrols were put out on two types of operation. Firstly, we set up OPs to watch areas associated with terrorist activity or individuals known to be active with the local PIRA unit. It was difficult country to infiltrate, since there wasn't much cover. We would walk in at night, sometimes two weeks before we expected activity. The second sort of patrol went out in response to intelligence reports of arms finds or IRA sightings. These were the most dangerous, as we would have to move in fast, day or night, making the best use of available cover.'

The OPs used in the first type of operation were carefully concealed hides, often located underground and with the top sealed with turf. In the second type, OP concealment relied on whatever was available, which was

Above: An Army Westland Scout helicopter drops off a patrol in the rural border area of South Armagh.

Below: A four-man patrol awaits helicopter extraction. Pilots of the Army, RAF and RN provide a 24-hour-a-day service.

often only a bush or wall. If an OP was compromised, the discovery resulted in a dash to the Landing Zone (LZ), where the patrol would be extracted by helicopter.

One of the Regiment's first successes in this new campaign came on 11 March 1976. Acting on a tip that Sean McKenna, a 23-year-old suspected PIRA member, was hiding in the South — in Edentubber, County Louth — a four-man patrol slipped across the border to arrest him. Two members of the patrol secured the outside of McKenna's rented cottage, while the remaining two entered the building. McKenna awoke to find the SAS in his bedroom. Marched across the border, he was handed over to the Royal Ulster Constabulary (RUC). He was tried on 25 charges and sentenced to 303 years in prison.

The same style of operation was used to capture Peter Joseph Cleary, a PIRA staff officer posing as a scrap-metal merchant. Cleary was in the habit of visiting his fiancée's house at Forkhill, just inside the Northern Ireland border. An OP was set up to watch his movements, and a patrol

Troops take cover behind their vehicles as a bomb explodes in the Smithfield area of Belfast.

snatched him on the night of 15 April 1976. They bundled him across the fields to the helicopter LZ but, as the aircraft approached, shots were heard. As the smoke cleared, Cleary was dead, hit by three bullets to the chest. At the subsequent inquest, an SAS soldier — wearing dark glasses, a navy-blue anorak and a polo-necked sweater — told the court that, as the patrol was lighting the landing lights for the aircraft, Cleary had attempted to overpower the soldier guarding him, who then fired three rounds into Cleary, killing him instantly.

A description of the car was logged into Security Forces computer files

A year after arriving in the Province, the Regiment once again demonstrated its value in Bandit Country. On 2 January 1977, PIRA men ambushed a patrol of the Royal Highland Fusiliers (RHF) at Crossmaglen, killing Lance Corporal David Hinds. A description of the car in which the gang made its escape to the Republic was logged into Security Forces computer files. Instead of abandoning the vehicle PIRA continued to use it for operations. On 19

January, it reappeared in the district, and an SAS patrol laid an ambush further along the road.

Behind the hedgerow, the SAS found spent cartridges and a pool of blood

As darkness fell, a young man carrying a sawn-off shotgun approached the ambush position, whereupon a sergeant, covered by a trooper, rose from cover and gave a challenge. The gunman raised his weapon, and was instantly shot by the trooper. The rest of the PIRA Active Service Unit (ASU) had been walking in parallel behind the other hedge, and they immediately opened fire on the SAS. In the resulting firefight, more than 40 rounds were exchanged. The body of the young man with the shotgun was identified as that of Seamus Harvey, a local PIRA volunteer. He had been hit by 13 bullets, two of them from his own men. Behind the hedgerow, the SAS found spent cartridge cases and a pool of blood.

As a result of these incidents six PIRA leaders had been forced South and another four captured or killed. For its part, the PIRA propaganda machine was working overtime to convince the Catholic population that the SAS were acting as death squads. Nor was the leadership slow to seize the propaganda initiative and turn it to their own advantage. When they executed a suspected British informer, Seamus Ludlow, as he was leaving a pub in the Republic, they claimed that he was an innocent civilian murdered in the Irish Republic by the SAS, who had mistakenly identified him as an IRA man. PIRA did not have to admit to an informer in its ranks, while the authorities were reluctant to identify Ludlow as an intelligence asset.

In subsequent years, there were other incidents that gave the IRA propaganda gifts. These largely resulted from mistakes made by the SAS while adapting to the new type of war they had been asked to fight in Northern Ireland. But whatever the circumstances they are nonetheless still indelible blots on the copy book of the Regiment — one particular occurrence caused deep embarrassment; another family heartbreak.

The devastating effects of an explosion at Ballycastle seen at close hand. Miraculously no-one was killed in this incident, and injuries were slight.

The first such incident resulted in a diplomatic row. On 5 May 1976, a Triumph Toledo saloon car, containing two SAS men on a snatch operation, blundered into a Garda (Eire police) checkpoint about 500m inside the Irish Republic. Two hours later, a rescue party of six SAS men, travelling in two cars and looking for their colleagues, also crossed the checkpoint. When the Garda men searched these vehicles, they discovered an assortment of weapons, including Browning pistols, pump-action shotguns, Sterling sub-machine guns and various knives. The soldiers were taken to Dundalk, where they were charged with the illegal possession of firearms with intent to endanger life and released on bail of £40,000 sterling. At their trial in Dublin, however, they were convicted of the lesser charge of possessing unlicensed firearms and fined a nominal sum of £100.

The warning came too late to avert a tragedy

A far more serious and distressing incident occurred in July 1978. John Boyle, 16, who worked on his family's farm in County Antrim, wandered into the local graveyard to search for some family headstones. There, concealed under a fallen headstone, he discovered a plastic fertiliser sack containing a paramilitary uniform and weapons. The boy's family informed the RUC, who quickly notified the Army. In turn the SAS was briefed to set up a covert surveillance position and to apprehend any terrorist that returned to the cache. The briefing stated that 'a child' had made the discovery, and so the Regiment requested that the RUC should warn the family not to return to the cemetery. But the warning, not delivered until the next morning, came too late to avert a tragedy.

The judge delivered a scathing criticism of the operation

A four-man patrol had moved into the area overnight, two soldiers taking up position in an old barn overlooking the graveyard, from where they could provide covering fire for Sergeant Bohan and Corporal Temperley, who were concealed in a hide close to the weapons. Early the next morning, they saw a young man enter the graveyard and approach the concealed weapons. He opened the bag, pulled out the rifle, and inadvertently pointed it towards the hidden SAS men. Without issuing a warning, the two men in the hide opened fire, killing John Boyle.

Two members of PIRA, armed with a German G-3 rifle and a stick grenade, pose for a photograph. Propaganda plays a vital role in the terrorists' war against the Security Forces.

A typical built-up area in the Province, demonstrating the difficulties faced by the Security Forces in 'cordon and search' operations.

It can be assumed that, like many boys of his age, John was fascinated by guns, and had returned to look at his find. Both soldiers were charged with murder and, in a controversial trial, evidence was presented indicating that the bullets had struck John Boyle from behind. Despite the acquittal of the SAS soldiers, the judge delivered a scathing criticism of the operation. The IRA had been presented with a major propaganda triumph.

Not all the IRA's victories against the SAS were to be won by words alone, however. In the area in which the SAS operated, there were some highly dangerous and experienced terrorists. Among them were confederates of Dominic McGlinchey, a renegade IRA man who was believed to be responsible for over 30 murders. McGlinchey had become the leader of the self-styled Irish

National Liberation Army (INLA), a small splinter group containing some of the most hardened terrorists.

Dustbin lids were banged together as a warning of the soldiers' arrival

In March 1978, Intelligence identified a house in a small hamlet outside Londonderry as a terrorist safe-house. The Regiment was detailed to set up an OP in a nearby lane in order to keep the house under observation. On the night of the 16th, two SAS soldiers in the hide heard movement along the hedgerow to their rear. Through their starlight 'scopes they saw, walking towards them, two figures that appeared to be wearing UDR uniforms. As regular units were not always informed of SAS operations, Lance Corporal David Jones stood up to identify himself, and immediately received a fatal bullet wound to the chest. The other SAS man, also wounded in the contact, returned fire.

The Security Forces were quick to react. After the two soldiers had been evacuated, dog teams and heavily armed troops followed a trail of blood that led away from the hedgerow. They found a prominent INLA terrorist, Frank Hughes, hiding in a gorse bush and nursing a wounded leg. A man infamous for the murders of two policemen had proved himself faster than the SAS men. The Regiment, dependent for the success of its operations on stealth, surprise and speed, would not easily forget their mistake.

Among the most demanding, dangerous and difficult duties a soldier can be asked to perform are operations in built-up areas, and the risks are multiplied when the operation is undercover. In the labyrinths of the Falls Road area of Belfast and the sprawl of Andersonstown, surveillance was a dangerous occupation. Cars and pedestrians were being checked at barricades set up by paramilitaries, and the passage of an Army foot patrol was habitually accompanied by the cacophony of dustbin lids being banged together by local women as a warning of the soldiers' arrival.

A slate pin would be replaced with an elastic band

When an excellent reason arose for the establishment of an OP within the sectarian ghettos, troops in armoured personnel carriers (APCs) would arrive in the streets. An SAS trooper, who was on service in the Province at the time, describes the routine:

'The recce unit, which might be as few as two men, would be hidden among the troops detailed to "search" the area. A house would be chosen at random in the terrace opposite the target we wanted to watch. Ten or so troops would pile into the building and distract the occupants, while the recce team entered the loft. Once inside, they would "mouse-hole" along the terrace until they were in front of the target. A slate pin would be replaced with an elastic band, providing a movable peep-hole, the radio would be checked, and then they were on their own. When it was time to come out, the unit would raid the street again and we'd just reverse the process.'

One such operation was compromised when a plastic bag that was being used by the SAS as a latrine leaked excreta into the rooms below. The house was emptied as a PIRA hit squad prepared to attack the men in the OP. Fortunately, the senior SAS soldier realised that the operation had been blown and radioed for help. The Army arrived in the nick of time.

The SAS had been given faulty intelligence: number 369 was empty

On 2 May 1980, such patient surveillance paid off when a house in Antrim Road, East Belfast, was identified as an IRA arms dump. An eight-man SAS team arrived outside number 369 in two unmarked cars. Operating in a potentially dangerous area, the SAS were armed with Colt Commando 5.56mm automatic rifles and Heckler and Koch MP5 9mm machine pistols. One patrol of four men was briefed to cover the rear of the building, while the second patrol would burst in at the front.

However, as the car stopped outside the door of number 369, the team came under fire from a window somewhere on the top floor. One of the soldiers also saw breaking glass and muzzle flashes from a window to the left of the front door. As the SAS stormed number 369, Captain Westmacott was killed by fire from number 371. The SAS had been given faulty intelligence: number 369 was empty, and the arms dump was situated next door. Eventually, Regular Army units and the RUC surrounded the area and the terrorists subsequently surrendered.

In 1987 there were 12 attacks on under-manned rural police stations

This action, though ultimately successful, shows the importance of accurate intelligence, and how dangerous it can be to get it only slightly wrong. The gathering of such information through surveillance and reconnaissance is an SAS speciality. They were far from being the only unit active in this field in Northern Ireland, but they did help in the work of other organisations. The senior intelligence agencies in the Province were the Security Service (DI5), which was involved under a mandate to 'defend the realm', and the Secret Intelligence Service (DI6), which ostensibly concerned itself with overseas aspects of the war. The latter was to achieve great success in disrupting arms shipments from Libya after the interception of the Panamanian-registered freighter the

This arms cache, including Soviet-manufactured assault rifles, was recovered by the Security Forces from the Ulster Defence Association, a Protestant paramilitary organisation.

Eksund on 27 October 1987, and the massive follow-up operation by the Irish Security Forces and the Garda.

Another body running covert operators was the RUC, which maintained a foothold in the intelligence empire with the Special Branch unit E4A and their own Special Support Unit (SSU): E4A gathered the intelligence that the SSU (now disbanded) then acted upon. The RUC units, accused during the John Stalker affair of implementing a 'shoot-to-kill' policy, were trained by 22 SAS at their base at Hereford, but were manned by ordinary policemen and operated under the direction of the RUC and, possibly, the Intelligence Services.

Military Intelligence was also active in the Province. 14 Intelligence Company (14 Int) was part of their operation as was Brigade Intelligence (Bde Int). It was with the latter that Captain Robert Nairac was serving at the time of his torture and murder by PIRA in south Armagh in 1977. His killers believed him to be not a soldier, but a member of the Official IRA with which they were on bad terms. Like the men in 14 Int, those with Bde Int were seconded

The Hiace van in which the terrorists attempted to escape at Loughall. It was raked by SAS fire and all the occupants were killed.

from other regiments of the British Army (Nairac was Grenadier Guards) and were trained, in part, at Hereford.

By 1987, PIRA had started to direct its campaign towards 'soft' targets. That year, there were 12 attacks on under-manned rural police stations, the better-defended being mortared from a safe distance. One tried-and-tested technique used by PIRA was to breach the outer defences of a police station with a heavy vehicle. When this machine, laden with explosives, reached the walls of the station, the bomb would be detonated, destroying the building; the PIRA Active Service Unit would then lay down a heavy barrage of fire onto any survivors in the ruins.

Shortly after 1900 hours, an eight-man PIRA ASU drove into the area

When, in April 1987, a JCB mechanical digger was reported missing in East Tyrone, the RUC went on alert. A watch was set up on various PIRA members believed to have taken part in previous attacks, and surveillance on the East Tyrone PIRA Brigade's quartermaster was increased. The JCB was eventually discovered at a remote, derelict farm. The nearest police station was at Loughall, less than 16km away. A surveillance team was inserted into the area.

The explosives were ferried into the farm in broad daylight; the operation was being watched by RUC officers. As the actual date of the attack was still unknown, the ever-patient SAS moved into Loughall. Setting up a 'box-type' ambush, men were positioned in the isolated police station and also concealed in hides in the hedgerow opposite. Other teams built hides on the road at a distance either side of the police station, effectively closing the box.

On Friday 8 May, the terrorists were watched preparing for the attack and the police station was consequently evacuated. Shortly after 1900 hours, an eight-man PIRA ASU drove into the area in stolen cars. Lining up in the road, they laid down a barrage of fire on the police station to cover the entry of the digger, which ploughed through the perimeter fence and continued towards the police station. As the explosive charge was detonated, destroying half the building, the SAS commander gave the order to open fire. It was all over in less than a minute. The JCB driver, along with other survivors of the initial SAS fusillade, attempted to escape in a stolen Hiace van. Within seconds, however, it was riddled with high-velocity rifle bullets; all inside were killed. The PIRA East Tyrone Brigade had been wiped out.

After cruising past the UDR man's truck, they disappeared

However, like so many other operations fought among a civilian population, Loughall was marked by tragedy. As the charge exploded at the police station, a white Citroen attempted to leave the area, and drove past the SAS 'stop group'. Believing the car to contain escaping terrorists,

the SAS opened fire, killing Anthony Hughes and badly wounding his brother Oliver.

The operation at Loughall was but one example of the new, streamlined operations being run by the Intelligence Services, the police and the Army. Similar success came in early 1988, when DI5 received information that a former UDR soldier living in mid-Tyrone had been targeted for assassination. The RUC immediately stepped up surveillance on the Harte brothers, who led the mid-Tyrone Brigade. But, once again, the time of the proposed attack was unknown.

Below: The aftermath of Loughall. The damage and the area over which the remains of the JCB are scattered give some idea of the force of the explosion.

Above: The body of Captain John Westmacott lies on the Antrim Road in Belfast. Westmacott, was the first admitted SAS fatality in Northern Ireland.

On 20 August 1988, while the investigation was proceeding, the Harte brothers and another PIRA man, Brian Mullen, detonated a bomb that destroyed a coach carrying the 1st Battalion The Light Infantry to their barracks in Omagh. The ASU fled South, tracked by the Security Forces. When Gerald Harte unexpectedly recrossed the border in late August, the RUC reckoned that an assassination attempt on a UDR man was imminent. The suspected target was removed to safety and a member of a four-man SAS patrol replaced him. During the night, the other three SAS men began a long walk into an agreed ambush position.

The next morning, 30 August, the target's Leyland truck was driven by his impersonator to the ambush point, where a breakdown was faked. The patrol began its vigil. It was hoped that, when the man failed to arrive at his place of work, the terrorists would come to look for him. The death squad arrived six hours later in a stolen car. After cruising past the UDR man's truck, they disap-

peared, only to return later in a second stolen vehicle, and open fire immediately. Taken by surprise, the SAS man acting as decoy jumped clear and the SAS directed a sustained stream of automatic fire into the stolen car, killing the Harte brothers and Brian Mullen.

The SAS have clashed with some legendary names among the terrorists

After more than 10 years' experience in the Province, and in particular in the Bandit Country of South Armagh, the SAS have become practised in their new role of taking the war to PIRA. During this period they have clashed with some legendary names among the terrorists — men who comprised a new generation of 'hard men' who had the same courage and audacity as the Regiment, but whose reputations had been built on acts of terror. But though it is confrontations with these men, whether it be in the form of snatches or shoot-outs, that hit the headlines, such incidents are only the climaxes to operations, the real essence of SAS work in Northern Ireland is intelligence-gathering — it is the only way to ensure being in the right place at the right time.

FIRE AGAINST FIRE

The rise of international terrorism in the late 1960s and 1970s soon convinced Western governments that they needed specialist anti-terrorist units to protect their nationals from the excesses of bombers and hijackers. Many countries were compelled to raise new forces to meet this threat; Britain turned to the ever-adaptable Special Air Service.

For the fourth time that day, he crouched, waiting for the earpiece of his headset to crackle into life with the controller's command to move. Both the rubber face-mask of his respirator and his headset were hot beneath his anti-flash hood, and sweat coated his face and trickled down his nose. He was uncomfortable and felt mildly claustrophobic, and his view of the outside world was restricted — to what he could see through the respirator's eye-pieces and what he could hear through his headphones. He waited, pent-up, for the order to move in.

Suddenly the crackle of static erupted in his ears, followed by the command 'Sections One and Two, Go! Go! Go!' Still he waited. There was a pause, and he could easily and accurately visualise the two four-man teams springing into action and abseiling off the top of the

Men on CRW training barge through a swing-door. The soldier on the left carries his MP5 left-handed to give himself the widest possible arc of fire.

neighbouring roof, then sliding quickly down the side of the building. 'Section Three, Go! Go! Go!' On the first 'Go!', he pressed the button on the small metal box he was holding, detonating a charge that exploded with a mighty bang. Although knocked backwards by the blast, he was up and moving towards the wall before the plaster dust even had a chance to settle. Debris filled the room, but close-to he could clearly make out a hole in the wall about a metre in diameter and around a metre up from the floor. He gave a signal to one of the three other soldiers with him. The man moved forward quickly, and lobbed a stun grenade through the opening. Less than three seconds later, there was an almighty flash and bang, and the building shook.

Pausing slightly, they aimed their Heckler and Kock MP5s

A second or two later, the first man was through the hole and halfway into a forward roll on the other side. He came up in a crouch, weapon held directly in front of him. There was only one target in the room — a terrorist. The soldier fired three well-aimed bursts down the central 'killing' line before moving off across to the far side of the room.

The other three men had now tumbled into the room and one joined him by the door. Pausing slightly, they sighted their Heckler and Koch MP5s and fired through the closed door and into the corridor. A second later the second man yanked the battered door backwards while the first tossed a stun grenade into the corridor. While he made the obligatory count of three, he cast his gaze high into one corner of the room. There, mounted close to the ceiling, was a video camera. Aware that both his actions and his words were being monitored, he thumbed his mike, 'OK lads, a big smile for the controller. And let's clear the corridor quickly, or he'll have us here all f***ing day!'

The exercise described above is one that is practised relentlessly by the SAS at their headquarters in Hereford as part of their role as Britain's main counter-terrorist force, a role that daily is becoming more important. There are now over 1200 terrorist groups according to the files of the world's intelligence services. Some groups struggle for control of individual countries or provinces; others, caring little for national identities, are committed to the overthrow of 'World Capitalism'; others attempt to install right-wing dictatorship by means of 'death squads'.

A blazing BOAC VC-10 on Dawson's Field in Jordan. This was the most spectacular of the series of airliner hijacks carried out by the PFLP in the late 1960s.

The modern era of terrorism began when the Popular Front for the Liberation of Palestine (PFLP) commenced a series of aircraft hijacks in July 1968. New, highly trained military and paramilitary forces needed to be raised to combat terrorism. They would need to be prepared to launch operations anywhere in the world in order to protect their nationals. Furthermore these organisations would, irrespective of national considerations, need to co-operate with each other, sharing intelligence, counter-terrorist technology and expertise.

'The range is very stressful...there is a tendency to switch off'

While other countries created new groups to combat the terrorists, Britain already had units trained in the guerrilla/counter-guerrilla role. The most adaptable of these was the 22nd SAS Regiment. The steady decline of Britain's overseas commitments during the 1960s had left the Regiment with the increasingly narrow task of training for special operations in an East-West conflict. The Regiment's commanding officer at the time, Lieutenant Colonel John Waddy, prepared a situation paper for the Ministry of Defence, which he hoped would secure a future role for 22 SAS. He suggested that the Regiment could have three roles in combating terrorism. These were: intelligence-gathering, responding to specific threats, and pre-empting planned terrorist actions.

The Regiment's early ventures into counter-terrorism were in the field of VIP protection. With its long involvement in Britain's 'colonial wars', it was ideally suited to provide protection for those friendly overseas heads of state who felt vulnerable to assassination. To meet this challenge, the Regiment created a Counter Revolutionary Warfare (CRW) Wing whose staff could train elite 'Praetorian Guards' or, with such forces as could be raised and trained locally, provide protection themselves. The CRW Wing was also tasked with the collection of intelligence on insurgent groups and on all aspects of counter-terrorist technology.

As the use of terror increased, so the CRW Wing was enlarged to provide instructors in all aspects of close personal protection and hostage rescue. All SAS squadrons were rotated through the CRW school between tours in Northern Ireland and overseas operations and exercises. During its period on CRW, a squadron would be expected to undergo training in all facets of the work and to provide 'Special Project Teams' for counter-terrorist operations, either in Britain or in support of overseas forces.

For the purposes of a hostage-rescue operation each 'Special Project Team' is divided into two groups: one group is a team of marksmen, whose task is to maintain perimeter security around the target; the other is the assault team, which executes the actual rescue.

Training at the CRW school lays great emphasis on Close Quarter Battle (CQB) skills. This is a field in which all infantry soldiers in the British Army receive instruction — indeed the development of CQB skills is essential for Fighting In Built-Up Areas (FIBUA). A standard British Army CQB range is a sophisticated set-up and contains remote-operated, pop-up targets designed to develop quick reflexes and to produce an overall awareness of the fast-moving battlefield. Using live ammunition, the individual soldier (or sub-unit) advances through the range, covering a 360-degree arc of fire. As the soldier engages one target, others are triggered to appear to his right, left, or even behind him. But the Regiment was not satisfied with these standard arrangements. An SAS instructor gives an example of how they can be modified:

'The range is very stressful and tiring, and once you have been round it a couple of times, there is a tendency to switch off. Having engaged a target successfully, some of the lads would forget to check their rear. So we had this idea of concealing a machine, opposite the targets, that fired high-speed tennis balls at head height seconds after the target had been engaged. If, after firing on the target, you spin round in a crouch to check the area to your rear, you don't get a clout on the head. It does tend to focus one's concentration.'

Exercises take place under conditions which are as realistic as possible

It was soon realised, however, that rescuing hostages held by heavily armed terrorists in, for instance, the cabin of an airliner called for more refined skills in Close Quarter Battle. Therefore a building known as the 'Killing House' was constructed at SAS HQ at Hereford. The 'Killing House' can be laid out and furnished to look like any of the vast array of targets the Regiment may be called upon to assault, from a government building to a suburban 'semi'. Here SAS soldiers learn how to terminate a hostage situation in the fastest, most efficient way. Exercises take place under conditions which are as realistic as possible, down to the use of live rounds and pyrotechnic devices. The assault team — the team which carries out the rescue attempt — is split into pairs which strike simultaneously at different points of the house.

A set procedure is used for entering rooms. The pair first take up position either side of the door. Then one man will force an entry, using a shotgun, while the second throws in a stun grenade, or 'flash-bang'. This device is 15cm long and 10cm wide and contains a mixture of magnesium powder and mercury fulminate. When the

grenade is thrown, the mercury fulminate, a percussion explosive, detonates with a very loud bang; the magnesium then ignites generating a 50,000 candlepower flash. The noise and brilliant light released by the 'flash-bang' serve to totally disorientate the room's occupants for up to 45 seconds, thus making the rescue that much easier to achieve. A modified version, the Harley and Weller E182 stun grenade, produces multiple bursts.

The SAS assault team enters the room immediately after the explosion. Until recently in 'Killing House' exercises, it would have contained a group of SAS troopers playing the role of the hostages, mixed with 'terrorist' dummies. The assault team had to identify hostage from terrorist immediately, and instantly take out the 'bad guys', while leaving the 'good guys' unharmed. Cameras

The burnt-out Border Police helicopters at Munich after the disastrous attempt by the West Germans to release the captive Israeli athletes during the 1972 Olympics.

inside the room filmed the assault and provided material for the debrief. A competent pair was, and still is, expected to be able to enter a room and neutralise any terrorists inside within four seconds.

This system worked well until an SAS sergeant, acting in the role of a hostage, moved unexpectedly and was accidentally shot and killed. An inquiry was held into the NCO's death and the the 'Killing House' was redesigned. The hostage-rescue area now consists of two rooms: one containing the 'terrorists' and 'hostages', and one which the assault team attacks. The rooms are connected by a sophisticated camera system, which instantly and simultaneously projects the events taking place in one room to a life-size wraparound screen in the other, and vice-versa. So, when the assault team bursts into the target room, it 'sees' the terrorists and hostages, and can respond immediately, firing at the images of the terrorists projected onto the soundproof, bullet-absorbent walls. At the same time, of course, the terrorists are responding to a projection of the SAS entry, and shooting back.

One obvious bonus of this new, safer system is that the terrorists no longer have to be played by dummies, and SAS men can perform the task instead, so contributing to a far more realistic scenario. After the exercise is completed, the films are re-run and, using time comparisons, the success or failure of the rescue can be judged. In an average training week, each man will fire approximately 5000 live rounds in the 'Killing House'. The majority of these end up in the walls which are coated with a material that prevents ricochets. For added safety, special 'frangible' rounds are now which have less than a quarter of the range of a normal round, and are designed to disintegrate into powder upon impact.

The Regiment's training is not confined to assaulting buildings

Traditional techniques for assaulting buildings call for soldiers to use grappling hooks or ropes to enter through second-floor windows, or make use of window ledges and drain pipes to climb onto the roof. Entering from the roof allows the attacking soldiers to fight 'from the high ground', and grenades, explosives and automatic firearms can be used to clear the rooms below. The building can then be cleared floor by floor, starting at the top.

These techniques, suitable as they may be for FIBUA, are often too slow, noisy and dangerous for a hostage-siege situation. The safety of the hostages is paramount and it is crucial that this phase of the rescue operation be achieved quickly and without the terrorists' knowledge. A less obvious approach than direct frontal assault must therefore be employed. For example, should the target be one of a row of terraced houses, the SAS could gain access to the roof via the building next door, or blow a small entry hole in a communicating wall — less subtle but still fast and efficient. The Regiment's training is not, however, confined to assaulting buildings. With the advent of attacks on commercial aircraft, several airlines gave the SAS CRW Wing modern passenger aircraft for use as training aids, and a mock-up of an airliner interior has also been constructed at the 'Killing House'. In addition, the Regiment has also developed techniques to end hostage sieges on London Underground trains.

Above: An SAS CRW trooper demonstrating the equipment used for abseiling. Note the leg bag which prevents the rope from dangling and advertising the soldier's presence.
Right: Directing operations from a rooftop.

Whatever the target, the SAS must have the equipment they need to stay a step ahead of the terrorists. The latest technology went into developing the special protective uniform worn at Princes Gate in 1980. It consists of a black fire-retardant suit, ceramic-plate body armour, and a combined respirator/Davies communications CT-100 system that allows for constant communication with the other members of the assault team and with control.

The SAS CRW Wing is always on the lookout to improve the armoury. For example, in the wake of the Mogadishu incident in 1977 the standard British Army 9mm Sterling sub-machine gun was replaced by the more accurate Heckler and Koch MP5 sub-machine gun used by the West German anti-terrorist squad, GSG-9. Indeed their special role means that the Regiment has been given considerable scope to choose weapons outside the range normally available to the British Army. Other weapons selected by the Regiment for their ease of concealment, fire-power or accuracy include the Israeli 9mm/0.45in Uzi sub-machine gun, the 5.56mm Colt Commando assault rifle and the Remington 870 pump-action shotgun. Interestingly, the standard 9mm Browning High Power semi-automatic pistol is still preferred by the Regiment for

close-quarter work and is used as a backup weapon on hostage-rescue missions.

The Wing also has its own satellite communications systems

Transport for the CRW Wing is provided by a fleet of fully equipped Range Rovers on permanent standby for counter-terrorist duties. In addition, C-130 Hercules transport aircraft, as well as Lynx and Puma helicopters, are maintained on constant alert for Regimental support by a Special Forces Flight of 47 Squadron RAF. The Wing also has its own satellite communications systems maintained by 264 Signal Squadron (SAS), which allow soldiers in the field to stay in immediate and constant contact with Hereford from anywhere in the world.

To support them in their CRW work, the SAS maintain a computerised database containing information relating to potential targets, such as architectural plans showing wall construction, window positions, passages and service conduits. From this information, all arcs of fire and

Left: Trialling weapons in a CRW environment. The Arwen is a five-shot weapon designed for anti-riot use but capable of firing a variety of lethal and non-lethal loads.
Below: The MP5K, carried by the soldier on the right, is the shortest of the H&K family. Very useful at close quarters.

assault routes can be computed using three-dimensional graphic images. The database can be accessed from the site of a terrorist incident by means of secure telephone lines, once again maintained by 264 Signal Squadron.

A 'Special Project Team' is on permanent standby at Hereford, waiting for the telephone call that will have it speeding to the scene of an incident. When the Wing was first set up, there were many in the Regiment who thought that the special situation which would necessitate their intervention would be long in coming — if, indeed, it came at all. But in 1974, terror arrived on the streets of Britain of a ferocity not seen since the Blitz.

houses frequented by soldiers. As time went by, however, the ASU became less discriminating, and bombs began to explode at offices, restaurants and Underground stations. Then, two weeks after two diners had been killed in the bombing of Scott's Restaurant in Mayfair, the terrorists inexplicably returned to the scene of the outrage.

On the evening of Saturday 6 December, a police surveillance team stationed near Scott's watched as a car containing the four men slowed down in front of the restaurant. To the police officers' surprise, a machine gun appeared and sprayed the front of the building. As the car accelerated into nearby Carlos Place, the two policemen sent out a radio alert before commandeering a passing taxi and giving chase. After a running gun battle with the police units that had moved in to try to block their escape, the four PIRA men tricked their way into 22B Balcombe Street, Marylebone, the home of a middle-aged couple, John and Sheila Matthews. As the Special Patrol Group (SPG) surrounded the house, the police negotiation team was alerted.

Members of the Baader-Meinhoff group hijacked a Boeing 737

The police were reluctant to hand over operational control to the SAS, and for two very good reasons: the hostages had not been harmed, and there was a strong belief within the police that military assistance should only be sought as a last resort. Nevertheless, it was thought that the mere threat of SAS intervention might have some effect on the gunmen, and so a report that operational control was to be transferred to the Regiment was leaked to the BBC and the *Daily Express* newspaper. The gang heard this story and it effectively ended the siege. The gunmen, if not the general public, knew that the SOPs (Standing Operating Procedures) for a hostage rescue were such that they would be very unlikely to survive an outright assault to release the hostages.

Thus the Regiment was only indirectly involved in the Balcombe Street siege. For its first major counter-terrorist assignment, it had to wait another three years — and then it was a foreign affair. On 13 October 1977, members of the notorious Baader-Meinhoff group hijacked a Lufthansa Boeing 737 en route from Majorca to Frankfurt. For the next five days, the plane was allowed to refuel at airports in various Mediterranean and African countries while the terrorists publicised their demands: $15 million, the release from jail of Andreas Baader, one of the

In August 1974, the PIRA General Army Council sent a new ASU to 'strike at economic, military, political and judicial targets' in Britain. The gang members interpreted their orders as instructions to create panic among members of the British Establishment. Their first attacks were directed at London clubs, Harrow School, and public

group's two founder members, plus the freeing of nine other activists held in German prisons and of two Palestinians held in Turkey.

The German government put its own elite counter-terrorist unit, GSG-9, on alert. In the past, GSG-9 had conducted joint exercises with 22 SAS and shared information about anti-terrorist technology. Now, they requested support and, in particular, a supply of the SAS' own invention: the stun grenade. Two SAS men, Sergeant Barry Davis and Major Alastair Morrison, along with an ample supply of 'flash-bangs', joined the 26-man German team in a converted Lufthansa Boeing 707 airliner as they followed the hijacked aircraft from country to country.

One was badly wounded but still alive when the shooting stopped

Finally, the aircraft was forced to land at Mogadishu airport in Somalia — out of the reach, it was thought, of European security forces. There the gang, along with the 86 passengers and six crew, awaited the West German response. If such incidents were not to 'snowball', there could only be one response, particularly as the gang had already murdered the 737's pilot. The German government instructed GSG-9 to plan an operation to free the hostages.

At dusk on 17 October, using a large fire on the runway (caused by a blazing oil drum) to lure the terrorists onto the flight deck, the assault teams crept towards the plane. Rubber-coated ladders were placed at the emergency exits over the wings and at the front and rear of the aircraft. Then the aircraft doors were blown simultaneously by means of explosive charges, and the SAS men threw in stun grenades. GSG-9 men stormed into the passenger compartment; the gang opened fire, wounding four hostages and one GSG-9 operative, and two terrorist grenades were thrown into the passenger's cabin. Fortunately they exploded harmlessly under the seats, and with precision shooting, the Germans killed all the terrorists, with the exception of one, who was badly wounded but still alive when the shooting stopped.

At Mogadishu, the SAS had assisted in someone else's operation carried out on the other side of the globe. Within three years they were to occupy centre stage in the west end of London. The first hint that the SAS were about to face their first major test of the techniques practised in the 'Killing House' came on Wednesday, 30 April 1980. A former SAS NCO, who had left the Army and was working as a dog handler with the Metropolitan Police, phoned SAS headquarters at Hereford and told them, informally, that terrorists had taken over the Iranian embassy in Princes Gate, London, and the Regiment might be asked to take control of the operation. Without waiting for the official call, the Special Project Team from the unit on rotation at the time, B Squadron, took the Wing's Range Rovers to London.

Earlier that day, five men calling themselves the Democratic Revolutionary Front for the Liberation of Arabistan had walked into the Iranian embassy and taken its occupants captive. The hostages included: 22 members of staff; Police Constable Trevor Lock of Scotland Yard's Diplomatic Protection Group, who was the embassy's police guard; and Sim Harris, a BBC sound recordist who was at the embassy to request a visa. The intelligence services soon discovered that the six terrorists — all from Arabistan, an Arabic-speaking area of Iran — were members of a Marxist-Leninist organisation based in Libya. It was believed that they were armed and supported by intelligence officers from Iran's old enemy, Iraq.

The Prime Minister, Mrs Margaret Thatcher, decided to put the Regiment on stand-by after discussions with representatives of the Ministry of Defence, the Security Service (DI5), the Foreign and Commonwealth Office (FCO) and the SAS — known collectively as COBRA after the Cabinet Office Briefing Room in which it meets. This recommendation was passed to the Joint Operations Centre (JOC) within the Ministry of Defence. This body is responsible for the actual deployment of the Regiment and is composed of representatives of the Home Office, the Foreign Office, the Intelligence Services, and the SAS itself. JOC issued a formal authorisation the same day, 30 April; as it did so the Special Project Team had already been in London for six hours.

The deadline was set for 1200 hours on Thursday 1 May

While the SAS retired to a London barracks to plan a possible assault, the police opened negotiations with the terrorists. Initially, the terrorist group's leader, Salim Towfigh (also known as Oan), demanded that the Iranian authorities release 91 Arabistani prisoners being held in jails in Iran. He also requested Arab ambassadors to act as mediators between the terrorists and the British authorities. The deadline by which these demands were to be met was set for 1200 hours on Thursday 1 May. When it became plain that the government in Teheran would not free the prisoners, the terrorists demanded instead the provision of an aircraft to take them, the hostages and an Arab ambassador to an unnamed Arab country.

Prepared for action. Darkened eyepieces to reduce the effects of flash, headphones to maintain contact and an aircrew knife to cut abseiling ropes — all standard CRW kit.

Above: *2e REP,* the French Foreign Legion's counter-terrorist specialists, turn their officers' mess at Calvi into an SAS-style 'Killing House' for a training exercise.
Left: The aftermath of the GSG-9 action at Mogadishu.
Right: All the terrorists were killed at Mogadishu apart from this woman, still showing defiance despite serious wounds.

Police negotiators stuck to their task — managing to gain the release of a sick Iranian woman on the Wednesday night — and by Friday morning, two deadlines for the meeting of the terrorists' demands had passed without incident. At this point Security Service technicians tried to insert audio and visual (fibre-optic) bugs within the embassy walls in order to allow the SAS some idea of the layout of the building should an assault become necessary. They were unsuccessful.

By late Friday, threats were starting to be made against the lives of the hostages. The terrorists were furious that their demands had not been fully reported by radio news and demanded that the request for Arab mediators be broadcast forthwith; it was. The next day British government officials held talks with various Arab representatives to try to reach an agreement, but without success, and on

Monday 5 May, the Iranian gunmen's patience finally ran out. Salim shot dead Abbas Lavasani, a member of the embassy staff. On the direct orders of Mrs Thatcher, the SAS were told to assault the embassy and free the hostages.

PC Lock was on him and had wrestled him to the ground

The assault plan was simple. Two four-man teams would abseil from the roof down the rear of the building to the ground-floor and first-floor balconies. A further team was to enter at the front of the building from a first-floor balcony which they would reach by crossing from the balcony at No 16 Princes Gate next door. At 1926 hours on Monday 5 May, the rear-assault teams, dressed in their now-famous black counter-terrorist garb, started to abseil down the back of the building. Using frame charges, sledgehammers and brute force, the teams broke through the embassy's armoured windows and forced their way in, throwing stun grenades as they went. As these exploded, part of the building caught fire and one member of the assault team who had got tangled up in his abseiling rope was now in severe danger of being burnt to death. He was cut free and fell onto one of the balconies — bruised, scorched, but alive.

Princes Gate. Right:The note authorising the SAS to take over from the Metropolitan Police. Below: CRW troopers arranging kit on the embassy roof.

24 PRINCES GATE
LONDON SW7.

AT 19.07 ON 5ᵗʰ MAY 1980
"I JOHN DELLOW, DAC 'A'
PASSED CONTROL OF IRANIAN
EMBASSY INCIDENT TO LT. COL.
H.M. ROSE

5 MAY 1980

H.M. ROSE   J.D. DELLOW

PRESENTED TO THE
METROPOLITAN POLICE
BY LT. COL. H.M. ROSE 22 SAS FOLLOWING
THE IRANIAN EMBASSY SIEGE
30 APRIL - 5 MAY 1980

Bomb scare on the *QE2*. A team comprising a Royal Marine Special Boat officer, an RAOC 'bomb-disposal' expert and a member of 22 SAS wet-jump into the Atlantic in 1972.

Meanwhile the assault team lost no time in starting to clear the building. The ground-floor group immediately despatched the terrorist guarding the front hall but the first-floor group nearly ran into trouble. Salim, the terrorist leader, was lurking on the first-floor landing as the SAS entered. The gunman took aim but before he could fire, PC Lock was on him and had wrestled him to the ground. The police officer then drew the 0.38in revolver he had somehow managed to keep hidden throughout the siege, but decided not to fire. At that moment an SAS man shouted 'Trevor, move away!' The policemen did as he was told and rolled to one side; Salim was machine-gunned by the SAS trooper.

As the struggle with Salim was taking place, Sim Harris, the BBC sound recordist, who had been with Lock and the terrorist leader on the first floor, made an attempt to escape the building; he was told to stay put by an SAS man. But at this point a smouldering stun grenade set curtains ablaze in the room where he was, fire broke out on the first floor, and Harris, fearful of burning to death, struggled out onto a first-floor balcony, thus becoming the first of the hostages to be seen by the public. As he emerged an SAS man ordered him to cross to another balcony from which he was escorted back into the building until the operation was over.

The rescuers called for the terrorists to be pointed out

Meanwhile in the telex room on the second floor where the majority of the hostages were held, the terrorists began shooting. They had killed one of their prisoners and wounded two others when men of the frontal-assault team burst in. By now the atmosphere in the embassy

Members of Pagoda Troop (22 SAS' CRW specialists) making their way across the Iranian embassy roof before abseiling down the rear of the building

was thick with the noxious fumes of CS gas fired through the windows by the SAS backup team. Unable to decide instantly who in the room was captive and who was captor, the rescuers called for the terrorists to be pointed out. Two were indicated and two were shot dead. Minutes after it had started the Princes Gate operation was over. Five terrorists were dead; the sixth was discovered trying to pass himself off as a hostage and was arrested.

The SAS' next hostage-release mission was quite different to these operations and involved assisting a foreign head of state whose family was being held by Marxist revolutionaries. Sir Dawda Jawara, President of Gambia, was attending the May 1981 London wedding of Prince Charles and Lady Diana Spencer when insurgents struck, taking over his capital, Banjul, and imprisoning members of his family in a hospital in the city. France called on neighbouring Senegal to despatch troops; the USA

offered the assistance of their counter-terrorist unit, Delta, but later reneged; Britain sent in the SAS.

The mission was entrusted to the second-in-command of 22 SAS, Major Ian Crooke, who picked two men, packed bags with explosives, weapons and a satellite communications system, and flew post haste, in civilian clothes, to Banjul. A contact enabled the group to miss out immigration and customs, and having located the Jawara family, the SAS set out to rescue them.

Events at Princes Gate were played out in front of television cameras

The first obstacle the SAS encountered was the security post outside the hospital, which was easily subdued, leaving Crooke and his team with the guards keeping watch on the family to deal with. This they managed by enlisting the aid of a British doctor, who convinced the rebels to put their weapons down as they were worrying the patients. The guards thus disarmed, it was no problem for the SAS to remove the family to the security of the

British embassy. With the President's wife and children safe, the SAS were free to organise a Sengalese push against the rebels that effectively ended the rising.

The Gambian episode received comparatively little publicity, while in contrast, events at Princes Gate were played out in front of television cameras and brought the Regiment much unwanted media coverage. They also brought controversy over whether it had been absolutely necessary to kill the terrorists. But if there was criticism of SAS methods at the Iranian embassy, it was light indeed compared with the storm of disapproval that followed the Regiment's next major counter-terrorist operation — Gibraltar.

In the autumn of 1987, routine intercepts of mail to the homes of known Irish republican supporters turned up a postcard sent from the Costa del Sol by Sean Savage, a member of PIRA. British intelligence circles were well aware that PIRA were seeking revenge for Loughall and that they were turning their attention to British military targets in mainland Europe. It was also known that a Belgian terrorist organisation, The Communist Fighting Cells, was providing PIRA with safe-houses and logistical support. The PIRA European intelligence officer was finally identified and put under surveillance. All the signs pointed to an imminent terrorist operation in mainland Europe and when in November a PIRA reconnaissance team was identified in Gibraltar, the authorities were able to deduce the target: the Royal Anglian Regiment band and guard. Further deductions, taking into account the probable target and the location — Gibraltar town — led to the belief that the attack would be made by remote-controlled bomb.

When the PIRA ASU, consisting of Savage, Danny McCain and a woman, Maired Farrell, entered Spain on

As the assault team goes in, supporting elements stand ready to give covering fire if required. The man on the left is armed with a silenced MP5 machine pistol.

The assault team going in. Ropes securely fixed, the troopers begin their descent. Each phase of the operation had been carefully rehearsed as timing was crucial.

Friday 4 March 1988, the security forces were waiting for them. A joint operation was planned in which DI5, the Gibraltar police, the Spanish police and the SAS would take part. The rules of engagement were simple: arrest all members of the ASU as they attempted to place the bomb. Firearms would only be used as a last resort.

At 1430 hours on Sunday 6 March, a DI5 watcher spotted Sean Savage in the Gibraltar town square. Savage was quickly joined by Farrell and McCann, who had walked across the border from Spain. Savage was seen to fiddle with the dashboard of a White Renault 5 parked in the square, and the three then made their way, on foot, back to the border. They were followed by the SAS team. The decision had been made to arrest them as they crossed back into Spain.

Meanwhile, however, a local police mobile patrol in the area, unaware that the SAS operation was in progress, was requested to return to headquarters urgently and, as they did so, turned on the siren of their police car. It has been suggested that this is what caused McCann to look back. Whatever it was that made him turn, as he did so he spotted the SAS team following, and reached into his pocket, where, it was believed, he was carrying the radio transmitter that would detonate the bomb. All three terrorists were immediately shot dead.

Even two shots may not be enough to stop a person.

The case has been the subject of much controversy. One area of discussion was the large number of rounds expended by the SAS in shooting the ASU. It seemed inconceivable that so many should be needed to stop three people. Some ex-members of the Regiment believe

The body of a terrorist lies in a debris-strewn office inside the embassy. All the terrorists bar one were killed during the assault; the sixth man was arrested, posing as a hostage.

that certain pertinent facts about ballistics have been left out of the arguments. One ex-trooper explains:

'When we were training for our guerrilla role in Central Europe, the Regiment placed great emphasis on placing two quick shots on the target. This was called "double-tapping". With practice, it could even be achieved using an automatic weapon with a high rate of fire. The idea was to make the best use of the limited ammunition available, and it was more accurate. In the counter-terrorist role, though, you can't afford to "double-tap". The close-quarter conflicts are so intense, you must be sure that your first target is incapacitated before you switch to a second target.'

In other words even two shots may not be enough to stop a person. This is a point, often not appreciated by the media and the general public, which is further brought out by video training tapes produced by the Americans for their law enforcement officers. These tapes are freely available, and their contents well known to professionals whose work involves firearms. They make it clear that there is no firearm or bullet in existence that is guaranteed to incapacitate a person with only one shot and indeed a lethal wound will not necessarily incapacitate immediately. In support of the first point, the files of the Federal Bureau of Investigations (FBI) contain cases of felons being shot with more than 40 rounds, over a period of several hours, before dying.

When this information is put in the context of the Gibraltar operation, it can be seen why the SAS expended so much ammunition. Implicit in the instructions given to the SAS team at Gibraltar was an understanding that the PIRA team should not be allowed to detonate the bomb. However distasteful it might seem, in counter-terrorist operations, the legal necessity of catching the terrorist in

the act, and the obvious need to prevent the crime, will always assume primacy over the humanitarian considerations of lawful arrest and trial.

Hostage-rescues and active CRW operations such as Gibraltar are the type of action which the public would perhaps most readily associate with SAS in their anti-terrorist role. Yet in addition to all this, the CRW Wing still performs its original, much lower-profile task: that of training soldiers in the latest techniques of 'minding'; that is, guarding heads of state. In security circles this is known as Close Personal Protection (CPP) and SAS participation in this field can be traced back to the 1960s.

Yemeni-trained assassins were killing British Special Branch officers

During the Aden conflict, Major Roy Farran (who had led Operation Tombola during World War II) developed a Close Quarter Battle school in order to select SAS operators for so-called 'Keeni-Meeni' work. 'Keeni-Meeni' is a Swahili phrase used to describe the movement of a snake, and it became a synonym, in both Kenya and the Middle East, for undercover work. To successfully pass selection at Farran's school, the candidate had to remove a heavy Browning pistol from the folds of his native robe and fire six rounds into a playing card at 15m. Operators who passed the course were used to hunt Yemeni-trained assassins who were killing British Special Branch officers and their contacts. In more recent times CRW Wing has trained the units of the Metropolitan Police responsible for protecting the Royal Family, Government Ministers and visiting dignitaries; the SAS have also replaced the police on occasions when specific threats have been identified.

As the SAS became more and more engrossed over the years in internal-security commitments inside Britain, groups of ex-SAS men formed private security companies to meet the demands of all the overseas countries seeking the Regiment's expertise. This was encouraged by the British Government, which saw in the scheme a further source of personnel for 'deniable' operations. The most notable of these private companies was the Guernsey-based Watchguard Company, set up by the Regiment's founder, David Stirling. Its clients were told that they would be buying expertise, not mercenaries. The firm subsequently worked in many African and Middle Eastern countries. However, when the British Government has considered a country's security too important to be left to a private firm, the task has been given to the SAS. This happened in Kenya in 1965, and in Abu Dhabi in 1968, much to Stirling's chagrin.

Occasionally, however, the activities of Watchguard have proved embarrassing for the Government. In 1969, shortly after Colonel Gaddafi seized power in Libya, Stirling organised a commando operation to free 150 political prisoners being held in Gaddafi's Tripoli prison, which was nicknamed the 'Hilton Hotel'. It was believed that these prisoners would form a credible opposition to Gaddafi's regime. In an attempt to maintain secrecy, Stirling employed ex-members of the French and Belgian para-commando regiments. However, the SIS (DI6) discovered details of the operation and, under pressure from the US (who at the time regarded Gaddafi as a bulwark against the spread of communism in the region), scotched it by making the details public. Another company that was run by ex-members of the Regiment was Keeny Meeny Services Ltd, which provided a team of 40 instructors to train the Sri Lankan police force's Special Task Force. It also supplied air crew to Lieutenant

Colonel Oliver North (before his impeachment) to supplement the ex-CIA Air America crews who were running guns to the Contra rebels in Nicaragua.

More representative of the firms in the business of counter-terrorism than those so far mentioned is Defence Systems Ltd, run by Alastair Morrison, who was the SAS officer at Mogadishu. DSL has provided security for business interests in Angola and Mozambique, and it also provides guards for US embassies in high-risk areas. Control Risks Ltd, a subsidiary of London insurance brokers Hogg Robinson, employs ex-SAS officers as kidnap negotiators. Among other successes, they obtained the release of two Lloyds Bank staff kidnapped by guerrillas in El Salvador, and that of George Curtis, vice-president of the American conglomerate Beatrice Foods, kidnapped in Colombia. The firm's 'kidnap-and-ransom' service is now being used by underwriters for Lloyds Insurance and many multinational companies.

So whether officially, or rather more unofficially, the SAS continues to be of critical importance in the fight against terrorism world wide.

The body of a terrorist being recovered through a second-storey window by members of the London Fire Service during the cleaning-up operations after Princes Gate.

READY FOR ACTION

In April 1982, Britain suddenly became involved in a conventional conflict of arms over a group of islands 8000 miles away. As the Task Force containing some of the nation's finest fighting units assembled for the long voyage 'Down South' to the Falklands, SAS squadrons were already on their way to act as the eyes and ears of the Task Force commander. Against them were the Argentinian Army and weather conditions of a ferocity that few, if any, in the Regiment had ever experienced.

In the early hours of 2 April 1982, from its position outside Port William, East Falkland, the MV *Forrest* reported surface contacts off Mengary Point and Cape Pembroke. These contacts were later identified as an Argentinian naval and amphibious task force, comprising the aircraft carrier *Veinticinco de Mayo* ('25th of May'); the destroyers *Hercules*, *Comodoro Py* and *Sequi*; the landing ship *Cabo San Antonio*; and three troop transports. The landing force included 600 Argentinian marines and a battalion of amphibious APCs (Armoured Personnel Carriers),

The Royal Marines of Naval Party 8901, their SLRs held above their heads, being led away as prisoners after the Argentinian invasion of the Falklands.

supported by various army and navy personnel as well as special forces commandos.

Defending the British island was Naval Party 8901, a small Royal Marines garrison comprising 67 all ranks, which would have been even smaller had it not been for the fact that it was in the process of being relieved. The Marines were armed with only standard infantry weapons, including 66mm and 84mm anti-tank missile launchers, and after a short action, they were ordered, on the morning of the 3rd, to lay down their arms by the Governor of the Falkland Islands, Rex Hunt. The governor, who was commander-in-chief of the Falklands ground forces under the Emergency Powers Ordinance of 1939, had decided to surrender rather than risk the possibility of civilian casualties. The first battle of the Falklands conflict was over.

On 5 April, D Squadron 22 SAS flew out to Ascension Island

The then commanding officer of 22 SAS, Lieutenant Colonel Mike Rose, first heard of the invasion on the morning of the Argentinian landings on East Falkland. His intelligence source on this occasion was reportedly, and some might say typically, a BBC radio news bulletin. Rose immediately set about informing the relevant authorities of his regiment's availability — and its ability — to carry out special operations in the Falklands. He also recalled men from leave and back from courses. While he set about convincing Army and Naval commanders of the benefits of SAS involvement in the South Atlantic, his men prepared themselves for the coming campaign.

22 SAS was admirably suited to the task that lay ahead. The Regiment's four 'Sabre' (operational) squadrons each had a boat troop and a mountain troop, specialising in skills which would undoubtedly be called upon during the campaign. In addition, one of the four squadrons was, at the time of the Argentinian invasion, serving its tour in support of British troops above the Arctic Circle.

On 5 April, D Squadron 22nd Special Air Service Regiment, which had been on standby at Hereford since the crisis first developed, flew out to Ascension Island. With them went Regimental HQ and supporting elements of 264 Signal Squadron (SAS). The following day they were joined by half of G Squadron so that by 6 April, the SAS had the equivalent of six troops available for operations in the area. Ascension Island was to be Britain's staging post for Operation Corporate, as the campaign for the retaking of the Falklands was codenamed, and over the next fortnight the island was the centre of intense activity as vital supplies were flown in from the United Kingdom; stores were brought ashore from ships lying off

the island; equipment was unpacked, checked and repacked.

Even as the SAS were en route for Ascension, Rear Admiral John 'Sandy' Woodward, the Royal Navy officer selected as overall commander of the British Task Force, was bearing down on the island with the advance group of ships, diverted from Exercise Spring Train in the mid-Atlantic. Simultaneously a carrier group, including *Invincible*, *Hermes* and the assault ship *Fearless*, had departed Portsmouth and was chasing Admiral Woodward south across the Atlantic.

The Falkland Islands themselves were not to be the first target for the Task Force, however. This fate was reserved for South Georgia, an island which lay almost 1300km to the east of the Falklands and had been taken by the Argentinians on 3 April. This decision to retake South Georgia from the occupying Argentinian garrison ran counter to the wishes of senior naval commanders. It was seen as a no win situation. Firstly the risk of committing a large assault force to the open sea far outweighed any strategic gain to be made.. But if a smaller force were sent in and defeated it would be just as damaging. Nevertheless there was a political requirement for action and Operation Paraquat to South Georgia was planned.

SAS teams would carry out recces around Leith and Stromness

Before the attack on South Georgia could take place, however, Rear Admiral Woodward urgently needed information on the enemy's strength and deployment at the island's settlements of Leith and Grytviken. The estimated Argentinian force of around 60 all ranks was expected to be concentrated in one of these two locations, and D Squadron 22 SAS, among others, were tasked with carrying out the necessary reconnaissance. The plan was that as a naval task force group cruised off South Georgia, SAS teams would carry out reconnaissance in the areas around Leith and Stromness. Meanwhile Royal Marine SBS (Special Boat Squadron) parties would land and reconnoitre Grytviken and King Edward Point. It was estimated that these recce patrols would last five days.

On 9 April, with 3 Commando Brigade stiffened by 3 PARA just leaving Southampton aboard *Canberra* on the long trip south, a party of SAS and SBS soldiers on Ascension Island embarked on the Fleet Stores Ship *RFA Fort Austin*, bound for South Georgia. The following day a task force group led by *Antrim* left Ascension carrying

An Argentinian commando, heavily armed and blacked up, watches as Royal Marine prisoners are taken away into captivity.

the remainder of the Operation Paraquat force; in addition, the submarine HMS *Conqueror* also deployed to the target area, with a party of No 6 SB Detachment, SBS.

At least once an hour, someone would have to go and dig away the snow

Five days later, the *Antrim* group linked up with the ice patrol ship *Endurance* 1600km north of South Georgia and started to close on the island. Cabinet approval for 'Paraquat' had still not been given at this point; in fact it was not forthcoming until 20 April while diplomatic moves were still being considered. Operation Paraquat began the following day.

Just before midday on the 21st, *Antrim*'s Wessex, a Mark 3 flown by Lieutenant Commander Ian Stanley RN, led the two Wessex Mark 5s being carried aboard the Fleet Oiler *Tidespring* through the steep-sided mountains of South Georgia and onto Fortuna Glacier. *Antrim*'s Wessex was the only one of the three helicopters fitted with a computerised navigational system and, in addition, the crews of the other two 'choppers' were inexperienced in arctic flying. The flight was not easy, but in spite of high wind speed, frequent squalls and poor visibility, the formation succeeded in landing the 16 members of D Squadron's Mountain Troop, commanded by Captain John Hamilton, onto the glacier. Atop the windswept glacier, crevasses and deep snow hampered movement and the men managed only 500m before darkness fell on the first day and they were forced to 'bivvi up'. It proved

Below: The Royal Navy Task Force steams southwards. With it go members of the Royal Marines, The Parachute Regiment and the SAS.

Above: A Sea Harrier sits on the flight deck of a Task Force carrier. These aircraft returned from the Falklands conflict with a greatly enhanced reputation.

to be a sleepless night for Mountain Troop. The lucky ones lay five to a tent, leaning against the sides to prevent collapse. The tents were ill suited to the task and at least once an hour, someone would have to go and dig away the built-up snow. The remainder of the troop remained outside, getting what little shelter they could beneath the equipment-carrying sledges, or 'pulks'.

The helicopter crashed into the ice from between 200 and 300ft

The following morning, Captain Hamilton, realising the seriousness of the situation and aware of the danger of frostbite and hypothermia, signalled *Antrim* requesting helicopter extraction. After a number of attempts, the aircraft had managed to pick up the troops and get airborne, when one of the Mark 5s was hit by a sudden 'white-out'. This is a phenomenon experienced in arctic flying conditions: airborne snow produces nil-visibility, the horizon disappears and it becomes impossible to tell the ground from the sky. The helicopter crashed into the ice from a height of between 200 and 300ft, the pilot managing to bring the nose up so that the tail rotor impacted first. The wrecked Wessex lay on its left side with its side door uppermost. The troopers and crew got out safely, the only casualty being one SAS man with a damaged back.

Recovered by the two remaining aircraft, the men were once again lifted off the glacier, only to have the same thing happen again. The second Wessex 5 crashed in a 'white-out', and the Mark 3, already overloaded, had

no option but to leave the crash site and return to *Antrim*, where an emergency casualty room was hastily being set up. Once unloaded, the remaining helicopter returned to the site of the second crash, but was unable to land because of the weather. However, the crew did manage to make contact with the two RN aircrew on the ground, and confirmed that there were no serious injuries. By this time, the men on the glacier had erected a tent carried in the second helicopter and had recovered further equipment from the wreck of the first. The Wessex 3 returned to *Antrim* once more.

Both units reported that enemy activity was light

A second rescue attempt was made later that day; this time successfully. The stranded SAS troopers, together with the aircrew of the two crashed Mark 5s (a total of 17 men), boarded the Wessex 3. The weather had barely improved, but in an amazing piece of flying, Lieutenant Commander Stanley managed to get his dangerously

Above: A wrecked Westland Wessex helicopter lies on its side on Fortuna Glacier, South Georgia. The landing, in appalling weather, was a near-disaster for the SAS.

overloaded helicopter back to the *Antrim*. The Wessex, which because of its all-up weight was unable to hover, was forced to fly onto the deck of the ship in a manner which went against the normal rules of naval rotary-wing aviation. Ian Stanley was awarded the DSO for his part in the operation.

It was now 22 April, and D Squadron were no closer to getting onto South Georgia than they had been 24 hours earlier. Like David Stirling before him, Major Cedric Delves, Officer Commanding D Squadron, realised that there are times when insertion by air is not a viable option. An attempt had to be made by sea.

On 23 April, five Gemini inflatables, carrying members of D Squadron's Boat Troop, set off for the shore from *Antrim*, which had crept stealthily into Stromness Bay. Three of the small craft made it, but the other two developed mechanical problems with their outboard motors and, having no power, were swept away in rough seas. The occupants of the three boats that did make landfall established an OP on Grass Island in Stromness Bay, about three kilometres out from Leith. The following night they set out to get closer to their target, but in vain; their outboards failed and they were driven ashore by high winds. Ice splinters then damaged their Gemini craft beyond any immediate repair. Meanwhile, the men aboard one of the two Geminis that had been swept out to sea the previous evening had been recovered. They had drifted helplessly for some hours in a heavy swell before a strong wind, waiting until first light before activating a SARBE (Search And Rescue BEacon), a radio beacon onto which a helicopter homed for a successful rescue. The patrol in the second craft remained undetected for longer. After being blown towards Antarctica, the Gemini came close enough to a remote peninsula to make landfall. Rather than compromise the operation by sending an unnecessary request for extraction, the patrol whiled away five days practising their combat survival skills before eventually signalling for a pick-up.

The continuing bad weather also affected No 2 SB Detachment. They had air-landed on South Georgia by helicopter and then marched along the Sorling Valley, but once in the water at Cumberland Bay, the heavy Geminis that they had carried for eight hours suffered the same fate from ice fragments as those of the SAS. The SBS too had to ask for an extraction. A later attempt at inserting an SBS patrol was more successful; this party carried out a reconnaissance of Grytviken, while the SAS maintained observation on Leith. Both units reported that enemy activity was light, and that they seemed fairly lax.

Sheridan was left with a grand total of around 75 men

Out at sea, Major Guy Sheridan RM, commander of the 'Paraquat' force, was anxious to begin the assault on South Georgia as soon as possible. The incident which had hastened the decision to attack was the engagement and disabling of the Argentinian submarine *Santa Fe* on the morning of the 25th. Sheridan was in something of a quandary. The *Santa Fe* had been reinforcing the Argentinian positions ashore thus strengthening the

Below: Personnel of M Company 42 Commando RM ashore on South Georgia. To take advantage of the Santa Fe incident, it was decided to assault the island with 75 men!

defenders' hand. The odds were further stacked in their favour because the bulk of M Company Royal Marines, the core of Sheridan's force, were aboard *Tidespring* which had been moved to a position some 320km off shore when first reports of an Argentinian submarine nearby had been received. This left Sheridan with M Company HQ, the RM detachments on *Plymouth* and *Antrim*, and a section of 42 Commando's Recce Troop, together with SAS and SBS troops not otherwise employed. A grand total of around 75 men; the men landed from the *Santa Fe* had increased the opposition to around 140. Nevertheless it was decided that the demoralising effect of the submarine's demise outweighed the numerical disparity and the attack went in that afternoon.

The intention was to demoralise the enemy with a show of firepower

The attack on Grytviken began with a naval artillery barrage directed by a gunner officer put ashore with an SAS patrol. *Antrim* and *Plymouth* put down fire with their 4.5in guns, working a creeping barrage forward to within 800m of the enemy positions. The intention was to demoralise the Argentinians with a show of superior firepower, rather than inflict damage on the buildings and cause casualties among the defenders. The scheme worked, and a heliborne landing three kilometres from the settlement by two troops of SAS further convinced the Argentinian commander there, Captain Bicain, that resistance was useless. The Grytviken garrison surrendered to Major Delves and Captain Young RN, the task force group's commander, signalled the Admiralty: 'Be pleased to inform Her Majesty that the White Ensign flies alongside the Union Flag at Grytviken.'

The chain of command had been complex

The following day, 26 April, Captain Alfredo Astiz, the overall commander of Argentinian forces on South Georgia, signed the instrument of surrender aboard *Endurance*. South Georgia was now back in British hands. The submarine *Conqueror* surfaced and transferred No 6 SB Detachment to *Plymouth*, and later that day, the remaining SBS and SAS patrols were recovered from Leith harbour.

'Paraquat' had been a success and the first step on the road to the recovery of the Falkland Islands had been

taken. It had been a remarkable triumph considering the unusual make-up of the force that carried it out: seamen, medics and aviators from the Royal Navy; Marines from 42 Commando; gunners from the Royal Artillery; and soldiers from the SAS — all with their own way of doing things. In addition, the chain of command had been complex and unconventional, with Captain Young RN having soldiers under his operational control and Major Sheridan RM commanding Army personnel, including Lieutenant Colonel Keith Eve RA, a Naval Gunfire Observation Officer from 148 Forward Observation Battery RA.

26 April 1982. Captain Alfredo Astiz, overall commander of Argentinian forces on South Georgia, formally surrenders to British forces representatives.

But for the SAS the action had not been completely satisfactory, given the Regiment's high standards. First there was the near-disastrous landing on Fortuna Glacier. Feelings as to the wisdom of this operation had been mixed from the start, with at least two men with first-hand knowledge of the area, a scientist and an RN officer, advising the SAS to think again. Furthermore the 'Paraquat' force commander, Major Sheridan RM, an expert skier and mountaineer, considered the 'natural' risks too great. He had recently returned from an arduous ski-mountaineering expedition in which he had traversed the Himalayas. In the event his misgivings proved well founded.

But the SAS did not realise at the time that they were being advised by an authority; other voices deemed the mission possible and these and the SAS held the day. The result was a fiasco. It seems that the Regiment underestimated others' appreciation of the severity of the conditions while at the same time overestimating its own ability to deal with them — and almost paid the price. Yet it is to the credit of the SAS, and in particular to their fitness, endurance and training, that Mountain Troop managed to

survive at all in conditions in which most non-special-forces personnel must undoubtedly have perished. And not only did they survive, they were still fit enough after their ordeal to take part in the main assault.

SAS and SBS recce teams were 'choppered' onto the Falklands

Boat Troop fared little better but it difficult to lay any blame for the problems encountered during the Gemini landings at the door of the SAS. The assault-force commanders needed intelligence on the Argentinian positions and the Regiment, air insertion having been ruled out, had to go in to get it by boat. Atrocious weather and sea conditions combined with equipment failure to give the SAS little chance; once again they did well to stay alive, let alone reach Grass Island and report. At South Georgia the SAS took a battering from nature, not from the enemy; in the Falklands proper they would show what they could really do.

The moment Operation Paraquat was over, both the Army and the Royal Marines special forces were hastened back to the main Task Force. This force, now at full strength with the arrival of the carriers, immediately set sail for the Falklands, while the amphibious landing force, 3 Commando Brigade plus 3 PARA, remained at Ascension pending the arrival of reinforcements in the form of 2 PARA, currently en route to the island aboard the MV *Norland*. On 30 April the 200-mile (320km) maritime exclusion zone (MEZ) which had been declared around the Falklands on the 12th was upgraded to a total exclusion zone (TEZ). Within hours of this coming into effect the Task Force entered this area and an RAF Vulcan aircraft, flying from Ascension Island, bombed Stanley airfield. The same day SAS and SBS reconnaissance teams were 'choppered' onto East and West Falkland to report on the potential sites for an amphibious landing by 3 Commando Brigade.

The choice of a site for the landing was no easy task

The choice of a site for the amphibious landing was no easy task. The principal requirement was an undefended, sheltered anchorage with good routes out from a firm beach. Selection of a suitable site depended on accurate intelligence information, but the Task Force planners had an ace up their sleeve in the form of a highly experienced Royal Marine major, Ewen Southby-Tailyour, the commander of the Task Force Landing Craft Squadron.

While commanding NP 8901 (the RM garrison on the Falklands) from 1978 to 1979, Southby-Tailyour had pur-

Above: RM Planning Group. On the left is Major Ewen Southby-Tailyour, commander of the Landing Craft Squadron; on the right is Brigadier Julian Thompson, CO 3 Cdo Bde.

sued his passions of sailing, painting and photography. During voyages around almost 10,000km of Falklands coastline, he had drawn up about 60 charts, made innumerable sketches of the coastline, and taken hundreds of photographs. With his unique knowledge of the Falkland Islands, Southby-Tailyour was able to provide the military planners with specific, detailed information about possible landing sites.

No roads, no tracks, just difficult ground

Armed with this information, the amphibious force staff aboard HMS *Fearless* were able to reduce to five the 19 landing sites initially identified as possibly suitable. After careful consideration and much debate, San Carlos Water on the west coast of East Falkland emerged as one of the favourites. Indeed it seemed the 'safest bet': intelligence reports suggested that there would be little or no opposition in the area, a vitally important consideration for an attacking force with almost no armoured support. The chosen site did have one major drawback, however: there were 80km of featureless terrain between San Carlos and Stanley -the ultimate target. No roads, no tracks, just difficult ground which would have to be covered on foot.

Right: Combat Swimmers of the Special Boat Squadron prepare to deploy from the airlock of a submarine. The SBS shared the recce duties in the Falklands with the SAS.

The final decision would depend on whether detailed reconnaissance showed that San Carlos was indeed undefended. Such information could only come from men on the ground, and that is where the SAS came in.

The SAS were exposed to the elements and the danger of discovery

The SAS patrols inserted on East Falkland by Sea King helicopter on 1 May comprised members of G Squadron 22 SAS, which had been hastily reinforced — even to the extent of taking men who had only just completed the jungle phase of their training. Their task, though not easy, was simple: locate the enemy's positions, discover his strength and disposition, ascertain his weapons and equipment, and assess his fighting ability. In order not to warn the enemy of their arrival, most patrols were dropped off around four nights' march from their respective target areas. Moving at night and lying up by day — often in water-logged shell-scrapes covered by chicken-wire and with an overlay of local vegetation — the men were exposed both to the elements and to the constant danger of being discovered by the enemy. The fact that no patrol was compromised before the main landings at San Carlos took place bears witness to the professionalism of the SAS.

The downdraft began to shred away the camouflage from his hide

Nevertheless there were a number of close calls. One soldier was lying up in a typical hide during the hours of daylight, when he became aware of a helicopter closing in on his position, which was situated in open, featureless ground on top of a ridge line. He remained motionless, face-down and unable to see upwards, while the Argentinian aircraft hovered close above him. The downdraft, caused by the main rotor at such low level, began to shred away the camouflage from the roof of his hide, leaving him exposed and feeling decidedly vulnerable. The next few minutes passed slowly for the uncomfortable trooper, but eventually the chopper moved off, leaving the soldier to quickly re-camouflage his position and reflect on his good fortune. Evidently, the helicopter pilot had been checking his bearings during a cross-country flight, rather than looking out for an enemy patrol, and presumably had not glanced directly beneath his aircraft.

Once in their target areas, the G Squadron patrols set up OPs close to the Argentinian positions and lived cheek by jowl with the enemy, observing his movements. The information sent back to the Task Force and Amphibious Group was invaluable; indeed it showed that the

Argentinian forces were greater in number than originally expected. The ratio of attackers to defenders in any action should normally be three-to-one in favour of the former. In the Falklands, the ratio was right, but it was the wrong way around. The Argentinians outnumbered the British forces by three to one: not good odds.

Meanwhile at sea in the South Atlantic, the Royal Navy was experiencing a period of mixed fortunes. On 2 May,

Shades of the Western Desert. An Argentiaian Pucara aircraft lies wrecked at Pebble Island airstrip, one of 11 such victims of the SAS raid.

the day after the SAS and SBS reconnaissance parties went ashore, the British submarine HMS *Conquero r* engaged and sank the Argentinian heavy cruiser *General Belgrano*. Two days later, however, the Task Force, indeed the whole British nation, was shocked to the core as a similar fate befell the Type 42 destroyer HMS *Sheffield*. On station some 65km off Stanley, the *Sheffield* was crippled by an Exocet missile fired from an

Argentinian Super Etendard warplane; she sank six days later. Also in this time the first Harriers were lost — one to enemy fire; two collided over the sea. Nevertheless the shortlist of landing sites was now down to three locations and on 8 May the amphibious landing group, now stiffened by the arrival of 2 PARA, sailed south from Ascension. The following day the amphibious staff settled on San Carlos Bay as the target; three days later, 12 May, 5 Infantry Brigade — one battalion of Gurkhas and one each of Welsh and Scots Guards — departed Southampton as reinforcements aboard the liner *QE2*.

The SAS were to raid Pebble Island off the northeast coast of West Falkland

So far the SAS ashore on the Falklands had been limited in their 'aggressive' activities to calling down airstrikes by ship-based Harriers onto Argentine positions and troop concentrations, and, in addition, to providing co-ordinates and correction for the naval bombardment of ground targets. Up to now, information acquired by the SAS patrols had been used mostly for intelligence purposes; now it was to be used as the basis for an attack, to be carried out on the night of 14/15 May.

The SAS were to raid Pebble Island off the northeast coast of West Falkland. The airstrip on the island was the base for Argentinian-manufactured Pucara ground-attack fighters, which were capable of carrying a wide range of ordnance — and a lot of it. These aircraft posed a threat to ships close to shore and would also menace troops deployed after the landings; therefore they had to go and D Squadron were given the task of disposing of them. It was to be an operation in much the same mould as the sorties carried out by David Stirling's SAS in the desert.

Initial recce was carried out by members of Boat Troop, which, landing by canoe, established an OP close

Below: The 19,810 ton aircraft carrier I*nvincible.* Harriers from *Invincible* provided air cover for the Task Force lying off the Falklands.

Above: The movement of supplies was a problem, given the lunar landscape of the Falklands. Here members of an SAS troop signal in a helicopter to transport stores forward.

to the airfield and confirmed that there were 11 Pucaras parked by the strip; they also set up a mortar base-plate. The rest of the squadron, under the squadron commander, Major Delves, were then flown in three Sea Kings to an LS (Landing Site), approximately 10km from the airstrip. The 45-minute flight from *Hermes* passed without incident and all three aircraft landed safely. Once on the ground, the men were given an on-the-spot briefing before heading off cross country on the six-kilometre tab to the mortar base-plate. Here each trooper dropped off the two 81mm mortar rounds he was carrying in addition to his personal weapon and ammunition. The squadron then marched a further four kilometres to the forward RV, where, now in their individual troops, they were led to their respective start-off positions by the members of Boat Troop who had previously recced the area.

Illumination was provided by para-flares from *Glamorgan*

The assault on the airstrip was led by Mountain Troop. When they reached the perimeter, they opened up on the Pucaras with smallarms, M203 grenade-launchers and 66mm LAWs (Light Anti-armour Weapons). Illumination of the target area was provided by para-flares fired from *Glamorgan's* guns and the squadron's own 81mm mortar. In the artificial light the Pucaras were easily identifiable and the troopers were able to get in close to rig them with explosive charges and hit them with LAW rounds.

Their mission accomplished, the troopers withdrew from the airstrip under cover of mortar fire and with naval gunfire support from *Glamorgan*. The enemy had been caught completely off guard and it was not until the SAS were on their way off the airstrip that they attempted a counter-attack. This came to nothing, however; the officer leading it was felled by a well-aimed burst of SAS gunfire and that was that. With the exception of one NCO hit by shrapnel and another slightly injured when a command-detonated landmine exploded, the SAS raiders got safely away. In addition to destroying all 11 aircraft, D Squadron had blown up ammunition stores and had cratered the airstrip's runway.

The Sea King was circling off *Intrepid* when something went wrong

The SAS returned to *Hermes* aboard Royal Navy Sea King helicopters. Royal Navy aviation ably supported the SAS throughout the campaign: helicopters inserted and extracted patrols, carried supplies and evacuated wounded. They also transferred personnel from ship to ship at sea, and it was during one such operation that tragedy struck.

On 19 May, just two days before the landings at San Carlos were due to take place, a Sea King helicopter took off from *Hermes*. On board were 27 passengers, mostly from D Squadron, who were being cross-decked to *Intrepid*. The two vessels were only about a kilometre apart, and the flight, which took off around two hours after last light, should have taken about five minutes. On arriving at *Intrepid* the Sea King found another helicopter on the flight deck and it was therefore necessary to stay aloft and complete a second circuit. The airborne Sea King was circling off *Intrepid* when something went wrong.

The helicopter suddenly dived and plunged into the water

Flying at a height of approximately 300ft above sea level, the helicopter suddenly dived and plunged into the water, seemingly after suffering a catastrophic loss of power. The post-crash report suggested that this may have been caused by a collision with a large seabird, which was sucked into an engine intake. Whatever the cause, there was no warning for the passengers, most of whom stood little chance survival. Having hit the surface

The Landing Ship Logistic (LSL) *Sir Galahad* lies in flames off Fitzroy, East Falkland. The ship was carrying Welsh Guards bound for Bluff Cove.

of the sea, the helicopter immediately filled with water, and turned turtle and sank.

Inside the confined passenger compartment the SAS soldiers struggled to get out of the stricken aircraft. They were hampered by belt-kit and personal weapons — always carried by members of the Regiment when on operations — and few made it to the surface. In addition, the men wore only life preservers and not full immersion suits, normally mandatory for such flights, although it is debatable whether such clothing would have helped in the circumstances: the cumbersome nature of the immersion suits issued to passengers in helicopters may have prevented more soldiers escaping from the aircraft. In the event, those who did were picked up within 30 minutes.

As soon as the Sea King went down, rescue efforts began. The Sea King's two surviving crewmen, the pilot and co-pilot, managed to fire distress flares, and the automatic SARBE began to transmit its signal. Another helicopter was launched and began an SAR (Search And Rescue) sweep of the area, picking up one man. The remaining survivors were recovered from the icy water by a cutter launched from *Brilliant*, just as they were beginning to be overcome by hypothermia.

At around 0400 hours British troops came ashore unopposed at San Carlos

It was a black night for the Regiment and, in particular for D Squadron, which lost many highly valued and experienced NCOs. Altogether 18 members of the SAS perished and with them two 'outside experts' attached to the Regiment: Flight Lieutenant R. G. Hawkins RAF and Corporal D. F. MacCormack R Signals comprised an FAC team, specialising in guiding ground-attack fighter aircraft onto land-based targets.

The Sea King crash was the worst single disaster in terms of lives lost to strike the Regiment since SAS operations in World War II. Nevertheless, despite the severity of the blow, dealt by fate rather than by enemy design, D Squadron continued its operations. The survivors, now out of the battle, were returned to Britain, and reinforcements sent to replace them were parachuted into the sea and picked up by the Royal Navy.

With Operation Sutton — the amphibious landing by 3 Commando Brigade and 2 PARA — scheduled for 21 May, D Squadron's next task was to carry out one of a number of diversionary attacks designed to draw the enemy's attention away from San Carlos. Hours before the landing was due to begin, the heavily armed squadron was landed by helicopter on East Falkland from where it speed-marched to Goose Green and Darwin, later to be the scene of a famous victory for 2 PARA. 'Shaking out' in line abreast to the front of the Argentinian positions they engaged them with every available weapon. Constantly moving their fire positions, the attackers created the impression that they were a far larger force than they actually were. The Argentinian defenders, thinking they were under fire from a battalion plus, did not once venture out to probe their attackers' strength, preferring, perhaps wisely, to stay put in their positions. The diversionary actions worked: at around 0400 hours on 21 May British troops came ashore unopposed at San Carlos.

The SAS captain continued to put down covering fire until killed

G Squadron, which was landed on recce operations on May 1, had now been at large on the islands for three solid weeks, observing the enemy and sending out long-range patrols. It was now joined in its activities by D Squadron and over the next fortnight the two squadrons worked both East and West Falkland, sometimes inserted by helicopter, sometimes by Major Ewen Southby-Tailyour's LCVPs. Now the landings had been effected, it was less important that the SAS conceal their presence from the Argentinians and the Regiment was able to carry out more 'aggressive' patrolling: a number of enemy patrols were ambushed.

The land war was going reasonable well. On 27 May a patrol from D Squadron was landed on Mount Kent overlooking Stanley and the following day 2 PARA attacked and took Goose Green and Darwin. Yet four ships had been lost since the landings began, including the Type 42 *Coventry* and the container ship *Atlantic Conveyor*, and reports were coming in that the Argentinians were moving troops onto West Falkland. Five four-man SAS teams were inserted onto the island on 5 June, one of which was led by Captain Hamilton, commander of D Squadron's Mountain Troop and a veteran of Fortuna Glacier and Pebble Island. On 10 June, while working out of an OP established near Port Howard, on the east coast of West Falkland, Captain Hamilton and his signaller were surrounded by a superior enemy force. They initiated the contact in an effort to force their way through the Argentinian circle and Hamilton was hit by enemy fire. Ordering his signaller to go on without him and make good his escape, the SAS captain continued to put down covering fire until killed. This was a selfless act typical of the SAS, where a close bond is formed between the members of a patrol. It was not the first time that the 'boss' had

British special forces soldiers in the Falklands. Note the quilted 'Chairman Mao' suits, issued as cold-weather protection, and the American M16 rifles.

been killed covering his signaller's withdrawal, and it is unlikely to be the last. Captain G. J. Hamilton, an officer who had joined the Regiment from the Green Howards only five months before, was awarded a posthumous Military Cross (MC) for his gallantry. The war had only four more days to run.

45 Commando and 3 PARA converged on the beleaguered capital

Since 31 May pressure on the Argentinians had been mounting daily as British land forces bore down on Stanley. 42 Commando took up position on Mount Challenger west of Stanley, while 45 Commando and 3 PARA converged on the beleaguered capital from the north, 'yomping' and 'tabbing' respectively. 2 PARA advanced eastwards from Darwin towards Bluff Cove as the Gurkhas mopped up behind them. On 6 June 2 Scots Guards came ashore to join 2 PARA at Bluff Cove with the Welsh Guards to follow. But two days later, as the Guards waited to land, calamity struck as the landing ship *Sir Galahad*, carrying half the battalion, was destroyed by aircraft with the loss of 51 lives. Nevertheless the battle for Stanley was scheduled to commence on 11 June and two companies from 40 Commando, held in reserve at San Carlos, were brought in to replace the victims of *Sir Galahad*. Meanwhile artillery bombardment and constant airstrikes by the Task Force's Harriers attempted to further wear down the defenders.

Fluent in Spanish, Bell had spent most of his life in South America

But means other than the purely physical were being brought to bear on the Argentinians: the SAS had long since begun 'psychological' operations against the enemy. Lieutenant Colonel Mike Rose, CO 22 SAS, based aboard *Fearless*, had embarked on a plan to bring about an early Argentinian surrender. He was aided in his efforts by Captain Rod Bell, a young Royal Marines officer born in Costa Rica. Fluent in Spanish, Bell had spent most of his life in South America and was a unique asset to Rose as he tried to undermine the defenders' confidence in their leaders. Bell had spent much time speaking with Argentinian prisoners since shortly after the landings at San Carlos and, tasked with building up a psychological portrait of the enemy, he had gained a considerable amount of useful information. Rose used Bell's knowl-

edge to compose signals and despatches to the enemy highlighting the discrepancies between the official Argentinian descriptions of how the battle was going and what was actually happening. The 'bare facts' were then broadcast or otherwise delivered to the defenders. In addition to their involvement in 'psyops', Captain Bell and Lieutenant Colonel Rose strove to negotiate terms of surrender with the Argentinian commander, Major General Mario Menendez. Direct lines of communication were established and negotiations opened which may well have hastened the enemy's final decision to admit defeat.

The SAS and SBS attempted to fire the oil-storage tanks outside Stanley

While these complicated talks were in progress, the final push on Stanley began, with the battle for the mountains surrounding the capital. The Royal Marines assaulted Mount Harriet and Two Sisters on the night of 11/12 June and two nights later the Scots Guards took Tumbledown and 3 PARA Mount Longdon. That same night, 13/14 June, 2 PARA attacked Wireless Ridge with the benefit of a combined SAS and SBS amphibious raid as a diversion. Carried in high-speed rigid raiding craft, crewed by members of Major Ewen Southby-Tailyour's Landing Craft Squadron, the combined SAS and SBS force attempted to fire the oil-storage tanks outside Stanley Harbour. Although driven back by heavy enemy fire, which damaged a number of the craft but only caused one minor injury, the attack served to underline the weakness of the Argentinian position.

The following day, 14 June, with a general ceasefire in effect, Lieutenant Colonel Rose and his 'delegation' (Captain Bell and a signaller) were 'choppered' into Stanley, where they discussed surrender terms with General Menendez. Within two hours a final agreement was reached, and before midnight on 15 June 1982, Major General Jeremy Moore, the land forces commander, and the Argentinian commander-in-chief signed the official instrument of surrender. This completed, the SAS group moved off to Government House, where they hoisted the small Regimental Union Jack which they had confidently brought with them from Hereford.

Later this flag was hauled down and replaced by a much larger version, which arrived with the Royal Marines some time afterwards. Filmed by a TV crew brought in specially to record the event, the lowering of the SAS Regimental Union Jack officially brought to a close the Regiment's occupation of Stanley, East Falkland. The SAS soldiers took the incident in their stride. Operation Corporate was over.

Major General Mario Menendez, Argentinian governor of the Falkland Islands since the invasion, announces the surrender of Argentine forces signed at 2100 hours, 14 June 1982.

PREPARING FOR ARMAGEDDON

David Stirling's SAS specialised in behind-the-lines operations; the primary role of the modern-day Regiment is exactly the same and it trains hard to enable it to meet its commitments in the anticipated theatre of mainland Europe. And there can be no let-up, even with the dramatic thaw in East-West relations, for the volatile situation in Eastern Europe and within the Soviet Union makes a conservative backlash and a consequent hardening of attitudes against the West an awful possibility.

'Mission: a night infiltration by HALO [High Altitude-Low Opening] parachute insertion. Aircraft type: a C-130 flown by SF [Special Forces] Flight 47 Squadron RAF. Jump height: 20,000ft. Oxygen required. Opening height for main canopy to be pre-set for 3000ft. DZ [Dropping Zone]: approximately 20km from the target. Target: an enemy radar installation comprising some half-dozen buildings. Aerial photo-reconnaissance suggests target has minimum security. On landing, regroup and move off towards target. Intelligence sources reckon little enemy

British armour on the move. In time of war, SAS patrols would relay intelligence back for use by ground and air forces.

Soviet armoured reconnaissance units would be the first targets indicated by the SAS — but it would not be the Regiment's job to attack them.

activity in the area between the DZ and the target, although small, lightly equipped foot patrols have been seen close to the radar site. Suggest establish LUP [Lying-Up Place] during daylight hours from which the target can be observed, and move up to the perimeter under cover of darkness.

'Approach and "eyeball"'. Study area for sentry schedule before entering compound and laying charges. Avoid contact with the enemy. Move out to PUP [Pick-Up Point] five kilometres from target. LZ [Landing Zone]: unprepared grass strip running northeast to southwest. Layout IR [Infra Red] lights for exfil by C-130 flying in with NVG [Night Vision Goggles]. When aircraft lands, detonate charges at target by remote before boarding.'

The above is an example of one of the many types of military operation for which the SAS regularly trains. Indeed this is the Regiment performing in its primary role, which is purely military, despite the general impression created in recent years by the media of the Regiment as a

unit dedicated to covert, clandestine and counter-revolutionary warfare. A major confrontation between NATO and the Warsaw Pact countries is still a possibility even in the era of Gorbachev. Not only is there uncertainty over the future of Eastern Europe in the wake of the revolutionary changes which occurred there at the end of the 1980s, but the position of Gorbachev himself is by no means totally secure. The Soviet leader faces political, economic and nationalities problems at home and should he lose the struggle and fall from power, it is feared that East-West relations may suffer a rapid decline if he is succeeded by conservative military leaders who do not accept that Soviet communism needs radical liberal reforms. In the event of such a conflict, or the emergence of an out-of-area (OOA) operation, the Special Air Service would carry out the types of mission for which it was originally raised.

Precisely how the regular Regiment, 22 SAS, and its TA counterparts, 21 and 23 SAS, would be used, is shrouded in secrecy. However, by analysing the potential threat, and by taking into consideration the specialist training and capabilities of the SAS trooper, it is possible to get a fairly accurate picture of how he would be employed.

On the outbreak of an East-West conflict in Northern or Central Europe, the Soviet/Warsaw Pact forces would probably launch an all-out offensive aimed at both devastating NATO's defences and destroying West Germany as a political entity. Such an invasion would be likely to coincide with one of the major WarPac manoeuvres that are held just across the border, or with one of the bi-annual troop rotations of the Soviet forces based in East Germany. Soviet armoured thrusts into West Germany would probably aim at punching through the areas between individual NATO countries' corps boundaries, while at the same time a series of massive airstrikes would be launched with the intention of catching NATO air and land forces by surprise.

The alliance's military planners would have 48 hours to recognise the threat

A surprise attack is the greatest threat faced by NATO, but logistical considerations on the Soviet side mean that there must be some build-up to the assault. Soviet military planners would have to inform their forward-deployed divisions of the decision to advance about 24 hours before H-Hour in order for these formations, together with their supporting arms and services, to move up to their start-off positions. The second-echelon formations would have even greater distances to travel to reach the frontier areas and would rely on the road and rail networks: WarPac armoured vehicles would no doubt be loaded onto tank-transporters for road moves, and flat-cars for movement by rail.

Although it is considered possible that first-line elements of Soviet/WarPac forces could deploy to their jump-off positions in 24 hours, a far more realistic time-scale is 48 hours minimum. NATO maintains a sophisticated intelligence-gathering apparatus, including satellites and border signals-monitoring stations, and should therefore receive the maximum degree of warning. The alliance's military planners would then have 48 hours to recognise the threat, mobilise reserves, and deploy troops. Among the first reinforcements to reach West Germany would be intelligence-gathering elements of the 21st and 23rd SAS Regiments. This is because, in keeping with current tactical doctrine, NATO's armed forces require high-grade intelligence to maintain the 'Forward Defence' concept. While the various corps commanders have at their disposal modern satellite and remotely piloted vehicle systems to gather intelligence — in addition to the more traditional intelligence-acquisition assets, such as air and ground reconnaissance units — it is recognised that specialist close-reconnaissance units are required to provide the hard information that the com-

manders require. This is where 21 and 23 SAS come in; they are Britain's Long Range Reconnaissance Patrol (LRRP) troops, or 'Lurps'.

Long Range Reconnaissance Patrol troops are capable of operating for long periods, with little or no support, in close proximity to the enemy. They work in small groups of between four and six men, often behind enemy lines, and are equipped with long-range communications facilities to allow them to keep up a flow of accurate, up-to-date information back to commanders at corps level. LRRPs provide these commanders with information on enemy movement, equipment, and weapons systems; locations of headquarters, supply bases and airfields; and much more tactical and strategically valuable intelligence.

'Lurp' units have been developed by most NATO countries. Such specialist work requires highly trained soldiers, which LRRP troops are drawn from their respective countries' special operations force units. For example, Belgium has had members of its Para-Commando Battalion trained in LRRP duties while Holland has entrusted this work to the Army Commandos. West Germany has LRRP troops, known as *Fernspaehtruppen*, and over the last 20 years or so, a bond has developed between these and the SAS, born out of mutual respect and a similar professional approach to their shared role.

Life in an underground hide can be extremely unpleasant

The LRRP trooper's primary role is not one of a combat soldier. Indeed, he must avoid a confrontation with the enemy at all costs. His role is rather one of observation, identification and the communication of intelligence, and to do this he must avoid detection. His fieldcraft skills must be exceptional and he must be an expert in tactical movement.

The LRRP trooper moves — when he moves at all — primarily at night. Part of his job demands that he get into a position where he can actually see enemy troop movement. This may involve digging a hide location from which he can transmit information back to his base. Life in an underground hide can be extremely unpleasant, as described by a former member of the SAS:

'Spending four days underground with three of your "oppos" can be incredibly boring. The main thing that actually came out of the exercise was how appalling this role really would be, because we were stuck down in this underground shelter for three solid days in pretty squalid conditions. It was the first time that this type of shelter had really been subjected to any serious testing by a full unit on a large-scale exercise, although small numbers of men, two or three at a time, had trailed the kit for short periods while on exercise in Zambia on an individual basis. But this was really the first time that the whole unit had gone down with all of the shelters as we would do for real, and it was certainly the first time that the majority of us had to become familiar with the kit itself. We didn't realise how bad it was until the final stage of the exercise.

'Exfiltration from the operational area was to be by air. The move out was undertaken by Royal Navy helicopters. They came in to pick us up and, as we moved to our helo and jumped in, the RN aircrew physically moved away from us and kept us at arm's length. We couldn't figure out why at the time. We had been out in the field for about five days, and underground in the shelters for about four. We had no idea how disgusting we smelt, because we were used to it. We smelt awful. In the shelter, we had to crap and piss into different bags which were then sealed together in a plastic bag. Do both together in the same bag and it is prone to explode. Before this exercise they tended to explode inside the shelter, a problem that has since been ironed out, but you could end up covered in the stuff, and with no real way to clear the mess up. We were also hot-bunking, using two sleeping bags between the four of us, surrounded by all our kit and with no room to move. The food was appalling and, probably because of the overriding stench, tasted awful. I'll never forget when we at last came out: the first gasp of fresh air after 90 hours underground — it was quite unbelievable.'

Many of the techniques are learned by the troopers at their parent units

Many of the techniques required by Long Range Reconnaissance Patrols are learned by the troopers at their parent units, but there is an advanced training facility in Bavaria available for LRRP troops — the International Long Range Reconnaissance Patrol School, at Weingarten. This establishment is commanded by a West German lieutenant colonel, and its instructing staff is provided by Belgium, Britain, Greece, Italy and the United States.

The school is divided into two parts: No 1 Wing, which is internationally staffed and conducts advanced training in LRRP techniques for NATO special operations forces, and No 2 Wing, which is purely for basic and intermediate training of *Fernspaeh* troops and is entirely German. The training conducted by both wings is of an exceptionally high standard and, in addition to LRRP

Soviet naval infantry (right), paratroops and Spetsnaz could be tasked with locating and destroying Special Air Service units.

training, the German hosts also run winter and mountain warfare courses for the other NATO nations.

The school at Weingarten tests a number of LRRP skills and updates the students' knowledge in several areas. The school's courses are approved by an international working party which co-ordinates the curriculum. The courses are constantly evaluated, a flexible approach is adopted, and improvements to the tactics and techniques employed by LRRP units are continually introduced.

Great care is taken to train the patrols in the use of codes and ciphers

One important aspect of LRRP operations is enemy recognition. Troopers must be able to recognise enemy vehicle types rapidly and reliably. The make-up of enemy vehicle columns and their methods of deployment assist a corps commander in assessing the enemy force's strength, com-

Above: SAS patrols can be inserted by any number of means. Deploying from infantry Armoured Personnel Carriers is one of them.

position and, ultimately, its threat. With the information provided by the LRRPs, he can identify the enemy and deal with it.

In order to pass this vital information back to their headquarters, members of LRRP teams must be competent signallers. Great care is taken to train the patrols in the use of codes and ciphers, and to equip them with the most advanced communications equipment available. Messages are never sent 'in clear', but are always encrypted first. Using systems developed during World War II by units such as Britain's SOE, messages are translated into indecipherable numbers and then transmitted on high-speed morse radios. The introduction of 'burst-morse' radios has greatly reduced the chances of a message being intercepted. Additionally, this equipment lessens the likelihood of LRRPs being located by enemy DF (Direction Finding) units. The 'Lurps' are valuable assets, and great care is taken to protect them. Occasionally, however, techniques and training, camouflage and concealment, are not enough; and hides are located and patrols captured.

'None of them wore any badges, insignia or anything'

An officer with a combat supply unit recalls an incident: 'I was conducting a sweep to clear the area for my battalion headquarters to move into, when one of my men — never the brightest member of my platoon — came up to me and said, "Sir, Sir, I've found a pair of binoculars." Now this in itself wasn't unusual. Kit, even costly kit like binos, occasionally gets left behind when troops "crash out" of a position. So I wasn't especially concerned, until I realised that this private had left them behind; he hadn't picked them up. However, it wasn't until I started to bollock him

that I realised that something was up. He told me that he'd tried to pick them up, but they were "stuck". He also mentioned that they were covered by a face veil. When he led me back to his "binoculars", we found that one of the more switched-on members of the platoon had placed his beret over the binos, which, as you've probably guessed, were in fact a periscope. Anyway, this was the first time I had seen anything like it. Of course, I'd heard rumours about SAS hides, but this was the first one I'd come across. They're pretty difficult to find.

'Well, we looked around the area, sent for another platoon, and after shouting down into the ground "Give yourself up!", or something like that, nothing happened until we started to dig. Then, all of a sudden, four guys appeared and took off. Of course, by this time the area was totally surrounded by members of my company, and all these guys were caught, but not without putting up a fight.

Below: The German Mountain and Winter Warfare School at Luttensee in Bavaria, where SAS troops train as Mountain Guides.

'Anyway, we caught them and tied them up. None of them said a word, except one — their boss, I suppose, although none of them wore any badges, insignia or anything. And all he said was, "Don't search us, we're carrying secret documents. Don't go into the hide, get hold of so-and-so" — at Brigade or Division, I can't remember which. Anyway, after waiting some time, this other guy pitched up, gave them a hard time for getting caught, picked up them and their gear, and took them off, saying to me, "OK, they're mine now, I'll take care of them." That was it. I must say, I'm glad I wasn't with them, as the guy who took them away didn't seem particularly happy with them.'

TA SAS troopers often come in the top five per cent

Evasion techniques are among the subjects covered in 'Lurp' training. Students at No 1 Wing, for example, conduct long-range cross-country marches, often having to avoid troops out searching for them. Carrying heavy loads, the troopers encounter numerous natural obstacles during these marches. Mountains must be climbed, rivers swum, crevasses crossed and forests negotiated — often at night, and all in order to carry out the mission. To do this successfully, LRRP soldiers must be extremely fit. Not only must they cope with the long marches, but they must also be able to stay awake and alert for long periods, accurately reporting their observations back to base.

The LRRP courses at Weingarten are both tough and well attended, and the NATO allies send some of their best troops to the school. Here Belgian para-commandos, Dutch army commandos, German *Fernspaeh* troops, US Special Forces soldiers and TA SAS troopers rub shoulders. The latter traditionally do well on the LRRP courses, often coming in the top five per cent. One point should be noted at this stage. Out of all the special operations force units which comprise NATO's Long Range Reconnaissance Patrols, Britain's contribution (21 and 23 SAS) is the only non-regular group. This comes as something of a surprise to other nationals, as a former British student of the school recalls:.

'We were some days into the two-week course when one of the American "Green Berets" from Bad Tolz [base of the US 1/10 Special Forces Group in West Germany] came up and asked us if it was true that we weren't full-time soldiers. It seemed to piss him off that we were doing...well, better than the Americans on the course, and we weren't professional soldiers.'

Left: Members of an SAS mountain troop meeting a visiting general during winter warfare training. Mountain troop soldiers are experts in rock- and ice-climbing and skiing.

Above: Instruction in how to prepare fish on a combat survival course at the Long Range Reconnaissance Patrol School.

There has always been an underlying but nevertheless deep-rooted belief within armies that the part-time soldier can never be as effective as the 'professional'. This is especially true of all-regular forces, such as the British, American and Canadian armies. All other NATO member nations have a professional cadre, but use conscripted soldiers,on compulsory military service, to make up the bulk of their armed forces, and consequently seem to be more understanding of 'civilians in uniform'. Whatever the prejudices of the various armed forces, British TA units have vitally important combat roles, and their performance in recent years has proved that they are more than capable of performing their assigned combat roles up to the required level. For a number of years, the SAS requirement in Europe has been provided by the two TA

regiments. The fact that, with the exception of the SAS, all of NATO's LRRPs are high-calibre professional soldiers, says much for the skills, dedication and determination of 21 and 23 SAS.

The international nature of the LRRP courses at Weingarten illustrates the spirit of co-operation that exists in NATO's special operations forces. New tactics and techniques are tried out, and ideas are swapped. Some of

Left: Armed with an SA 80 and wearing a dry-suit, a trooper demonstrates infiltration by water.
Above: Camouflage and concealment: vital skills which must be mastered by all SAS troopers.

these methods are quite unusual. The British LRRP school graduate continues:

'Apart from the US Special Forces, there were Belgians and Dutchmen on our course. We all got on well together, and it was interesting to see the different ways we operated. SOPs weren't all that different, but you did pick up new points which were of value. One incident I remember happened at the end of the course, when we had our slap-up "end-of-training" dinner. We had been promised a great meal, but in the event this consisted of us being given live animals to kill and cook. Two of the "cloggies" [the Dutch army commandos] had this interesting technique of mesmerising chickens. First you hold the chicken down — this method requires two of you then you counter-rotate a finger each side of its head in front of its eyes. It sounds crazy, I know, but what happens is the chicken concentrates on the fingers, gets confused, and just stops where it

is. You can walk off, come back 10 minutes later, and the chicken's still there, looking confused. The second method is to extend the chicken's neck with is head resting on the ground, and then draw your finger away from its beak in a straight line. Then it just lies there, wondering where your finger's got to. It sounds strange, and I don't know what practical application it's got, but it actually works. I suppose, by immobilising one chicken, you're then at liberty to do the same to other birds, eventually knocking out the entire coop. I've tried the same technique on women, but it only seems to work with chickens.'

A patrol might have to live on what it could find in the countryside

Living off the land is a skill which must be mastered. Without support, often behind enemy lines, patrols risk running short of supplies. Teams go out laden with special-to-task equipment — such as radios, weapons and ammunition — and rations take a back seat. In wartime a patrol might have to live for extended periods on what it could find in the surrounding countryside.

The LRRP courses and competitions are not the only opportunities that members of the SAS get to train along-side their NATO counterparts. The German 1st Mountain Division runs a demanding course at the *Gebirgs- und Winterkampf Schule* (Mountain and Winter Warfare School) at Luttensee, near Mittenwald in Bavaria. The *Heeresbergführer* (Army Mountain Guide) course is one of the longest and most arduous courses run by the *Bundeswehr*. Divided into a 17-week summer 'term' and a 15-week winter 'term', the course is open to suitable NCOs and junior officers, and is regularly attended by members of 22 SAS. The task of the qualified Mountain Guide is similar to that of the Royal Marine's Mountain Leader (ML). He must be capable of advising commanders at all levels on all aspects of mountain warfare. In addition, he must be an able instructor, capable of passing on his skills to other members of his unit.

Above: A trooper on lookout duty as charges are laid on a railway line during target attack. SAS troopers are taught exactly where to place explosives for maximum effect.
Right: Swimmers place charges during diver training at HMS Haslar.

The course begins at Luttensee with an initial selection week, followed by five weeks of intensive rock training at Oberreintal on the Wendelstein. Living in tents high up in the Bavarian Alps near the ZugSpitze, Germany's highest mountain, the troops become acclimatised and spend up to 10 hours a day on climbs up to Grade 5. From Oberreintal, the course move to Chamonix in the French Alps, where they get to grips with the ice-climbing techniques before attempting a peak in the Mont Blanc area. This difficult ascent must be achieved if the students are to remain on the *Heeresbergführer* course. The summer

phase culminates with a tour across the Dolomites and a traverse of Watzmann eastern face. By the 'end of term', the initial training intake of between 20 and 25 men will have been reduced to between 10 and 15, and the ratio of instructors to pupils will be at least one-to-three.

After a brief break for Christmas, winter training begins in earnest. Skiing is one of the aspects which causes most difficulties for members of 22 SAS. Often skiing for the first time in their lives, they have to keep up with native Bavarians who have been on skis since the age of four. This disadvantage is realised by the DS (Directing Staff), and extra tuition is given where required.

The 'victim' waits while his colleagues flatten the surrounding area

While getting to grips with the 'planks and poles', the members of the course are introduced to the tactical aspects of mountain-warfare operations. However, the German Mountain Guide course devotes less time to applied combat training than does the Mountain Leader (ML) course run by the Royal Marines Mountain and Arctic Warfare Cadre (M&AWC). The West Germans concentrate on the technical skills required for mountain operations, paying special attention to casualty evacuation, high-altitude medicine and mountain rescue, including avalanche rescue. This entails a volunteer being

Right: Aerial resupply for SAS troops, provided courtesy of the RAF and RCT Air Despatch Squadron.
Below: An American Bradley bearing the mark of a nocturnal visit by 'unfriendly' special forces during an exercise.

buried two to three metres under the snow, equipped with only a sleeping bag, radio, thermos flask and torch. Here the luckless 'victim' waits while his colleagues flatten the surrounding area to disguise the scent. Then, with the aid of a dog and poles, they set out to recover him. Officers and foreigners are the favoured 'volunteers' for this special treat!

After six weeks of ski training, all students must pass the West German Ski Association's Instructors test. This is particularly demanding, especially for relatively inexperienced skiers. But the standard of instruction is exceptionally high, and the students have already spent a month on skis, doing very little but going up and down mountains. Success in this test means a further three to four weeks on a high Alpine course in the Gran Paradiso region of Italy, ending with an extended ski-march patrol across a series of peaks of up to nearly 10,000ft. From Italy it is back to Luttensee for the final test and, for the successful, the award of *Heeresbergfuhrer* certificates and badges. Qualified Guides are respected throughout the international mountaineering community, civil and military.

The Mountain Guide course is both difficult and demanding, but it enables 22 SAS to train high-quality instructors who can then pass on their hard-earned knowledge to the Regiment's mountain troops. Expertise in the field of mountain and arctic warfare is valuable within the Special Air Service Regiment since SAS units act as Individual Unit Reinforcements to various regions of ACE (Allied Command Europe) as part of NATO's specialist reinforcements to SACEUR (Supreme Allied Command, EURope). In effect this means that the Regiment can deploy to any geographical area where its multi-faceted talents are required, including the Arctic. With this in mind, every year elements of the Regiment deploy to Norway for a series of winter warfare exercises.

Precisely what the SAS would do in the event of an East-West conflict — what missions they would conduct, and to where they would deploy — is something known only to the SAS and senior military planners, but some speculation is possible. A Soviet attack on the West would undoubtedly lead to a concentration of Warsaw Pact armies in the East German transport system and this

offers plenty of scope to Special Air Service units bent on disrupting the movement of enemy troops. For a start there are eight dual-tracked railway lines running from the Soviet Union to East Germany, each capable of transporting half a Soviet division a day. On top of this there are over 13000km of single-tracked railway.

Other possible targets include the many major roads, which are also ideal for large-scale troop movement. There are over 1400km of four-lane autobahn in East Germany, with innumerable bridges which could be selected as targets. But bridges, both road and rail, would be heavily guarded and difficult to destroy from the ground — as would their approaches — but they would still be vulnerable to air-ground and missile attack. The SAS task would therefore not be sabotage. According to recent proposals put forward by advocates of the US Army 'Airland Battle' concept and by SACEUR, in such a situation small parties of SAS soldiers could be inserted by means of HALO or low-flying aircraft, such as a small, high-speed helicopter. Their job would be to identify a target and indicate the best method of taking it out.

Regardless, however, of the method used to destroy the target, whether it be 'hands-on' or 'hands-off', the success of the mission depends on the ability of the individual SAS operative. Stringent selection procedures, a punishing training programme and practical experience in a wide range of personal and patrol skills assure the SAS a very good chance of achieving their wartime aims, whatever they may be.

Left: The highly sophisticated equipment and weaponry used in modern CRW operations.
Below: The more traditional equipment of the special forces soldier laying an ambush in the conventional role.

KEEPING UP TO SCRATCH

The SAS are renowned for their fitness — and quite rightly. But there is more to the Regiment's training than runs and circuits. From selection to being 'badged', a prospective SAS soldier follows one of the most varied and thorough courses of military training in the world. And it doesn't stop there! Throughout his service with the Regiment, he never stops training; there is always something new to learn. Indeed it is stressed by the Regiment itself that there is no such thing as a fully trained SAS soldier.

Out of the mist staggered a lone soldier, bowed down under the weight of a 25kg Special Air Service bergen rucksack topped with a bright orange marker panel. Soaked through, he made his way up the slippery trail — little more than a sheep track — until he reached the cairn. A pile of grey-white stones, contrasting sharply with the black, peat-like earth, the cairn was significant only because it was marked on the soldier's 1:50,000-scale map.

The soldier double-checked his map, studied his issue prismatic compass, and looked back the way he had come up the mountain. The visibility was worse now, down to about 30m, and the path he had taken over the crest and onto the small plateau had vanished in the mist. Soaked through from the damp air and the occasional, sudden rain squalls, the soldier shivered a couple of times before moving off downwind. There, in a slight hollow and scarcely protected from the elements, stood a hooped, green 'bivvi-bag'. The soldier walked across to the shelter and tapped on it.

The assault course on Sennybridge Training Area where SAS recruits spend time during selection.

137

Inside, a well-wrapped member of the SAS selection course's Directing Staff (DS) finished pouring hot coffee from a thermos into a plastic cup before unzipping the front of his bivvi-bag. 'Name?', he asked. The soldier told him and the instructor checked his list until he found it. When he did he discovered that this man was an officer, a 'Rupert'. The instructor marked a cross beside the name, and then confirmed that the lieutenant knew exactly where he was and was capable of continuing the march, before giving him the grid reference for the next RV (RendezVous). The exhausted officer pointed out the next RV on the map with a blade of grass he had pulled up for the purpose. Then, after accepting a quick swig of the by now tepid coffee, he rose stiffly and shrugged his bergen into a less uncomfortable position.

'You'd better get going,' suggested the man in the bivvi-bag; 'you've got some catching-up to do if you want to make it.' With that, the Rupert set off back down the mountain, wondering why he had not been asked any demanding tactical questions; if he would make it to the next RV within the time; and what would happen then. Most of all, perhaps, he was wondering what folly had induced him to apply to join the SAS in the first place. For his current state of extreme physical exhaustion and mental confusion were all part-and-parcel of the Regiment's notorious selection process; a process which has been a major contributory factor in 22 SAS' many successes since its formation in Malaya in 1952.

Volunteers must have a minimum of three years and three months to serve

The Special Air Service is made up of volunteers from all arms and corps of the British Army; it also has a small number of Royal Air Force personnel, who come mainly from the RAF Regiment. Unlike several of the world's special operations forces, it is impossible to enter the SAS directly, and each volunteer must have served with a 'regular' corps or regiment, and gained a good grounding in his corps or regimental skills, before he can offer himself for service. Most volunteers for the SAS are in their mid-20s and the average age of soldiers serving with the squadrons is usually around 27 — although commissioned officers can be accepted any time between the ages of 22 and 34 years and senior non-commissioned officers and junior ranks are eligible between 19 and 34. One stipulation is that volunteers must have a minimum of three years and three months left to serve from the date that, if successful, they pass SAS selection.

Gaining acceptance and then passing SAS selection and continuation training is a tiring and lengthy process that only the most determined candidates survive. Having expressed an interest in joining the Regiment, the man must first of all complete the relevant documentation at his unit. There then follows a short acquaintance visit to the SAS Regimental Headquarters at Hereford during which he will see the recruitment video explaining the Regiment's role, organisation and training. If he is still interested in going for selection, the candidate returns to his parent unit where he undergoes a check-up from his own Regimental Medical Officer (RMO). Assuming he is passed fit, the candidate then completes further documentation and then waits until there is a space on the selection course (run twice a year: one in the summer, one in the winter, regardless of the weather). When a vacancy arises, he will be called to Hereford.

What is not flexible is the standard that must be achieved and maintained

When the prospective trooper or officer arrives at Hereford, he will have at least an inkling of what is expected of him over the next month, having already paid the short acquaintance visit to the Regiment. The programme commences with the customary course introduction, followed by the final round of documentation and the issue of required kit. The formalities completed, selection begins.

The modern SAS selection course is based on that designed by Major John Woodhouse when he returned from Malaya in 1953. His programme, in turn, owed something to the training devised by David Stirling in the Western Desert during World War II. This continuity is possible because the Special Air Service still requires the same type of soldier as it did in the Desert and in Malaya. Like so many of the activities conducted by the Regiment, the selection programme is, within certain limits, flexible. What is not flexible, however, is the standard that must be achieved and maintained.

Training Wing's mission is to select and train the best men for the job

The programme is conducted by Training Wing 22 SAS, whose long-standing motto — 'Train Hard, Fight Easy' — still applies. Based at Stirling Lines, Hereford, Training Wing is a team of experienced Regimental commissioned and non-commissioned officers whose sole mission is to select and train the best men for the job. They make their choice on the basis of a man's performance during a

A soldier nearing the top of Pen-y-Fan. The 'Fan Dance', the final march on selection, is named after this, the highest peak in the Brecon Beacons.

build-up period — two weeks for officers, three weeks for soldiers — and a Test Week, a series of solo forced marches across the inhospitable landscapes of the South Welsh mountains. The instructors look for particular qualities in a potential recruit, one of the most important of which is a high level of physical fitness and stamina.

The marches increase in difficulty as the weight carried becomes greater

Fitness is initially tested upon arrival at Hereford with a series of road runs. All contenders at selection must be capable of passing the standard Battle Fitness Test (BFT) in the time required for infantry/airborne soldiers. This involves a one-and-a-half-mile group run in 13 minutes,

Above: A patrol awaits the arrival of a Sea King helicopter. 'Choppers', so important to SAS operations in the Falklands, can be no less welcome a sight on a British moor.

followed by a solo run of the same distance in 11.5 minutes. But the BFT is only the basic requirement; a very high overall standard of fitness is required when the soldier first joins the course. This is then built up progressively during a number of group cross-country marches over the mountainous countryside. These marches gradually increase in difficulty as the weight carried becomes greater and the groups themselves smaller, until eventually the men are on their own.

To make sure that they are near the right level of fitness to start with, many candidates prepare themselves for the event for some months beforehand. They go out on hill marches and perhaps actually walk over the Brecon Beacons and Black Mountains, the area in Wales in which SAS selection is conducted. Some lucky volunteers will get time off for this; others have to take leave.

More important still are personal qualities and character

Most volunteers find SAS selection and continuation training the most physically demanding periods of their lives. Nevertheless, much more than fitness is tested and a man's physical capacity alone is not enough to get him through the course. Certain skills — map-reading and land navigation, for example — are absolutely essential to the aspiring SAS man, but more important still are the individual's personal qualities and character. The Special Air Service requires soldiers who are self-confident and self-reliant and have the ability to endure extreme physical hardship and to carry on regardless.

This latter quality is to a large extent dependent on a soldier's motivation; something that is, in fact, sometimes put to the test when a man first decides to try for selection and informs his unit. Although a candidate's application for SAS selection has to be forwarded to Hereford, no platoon or company commander wants to lose a good officer, NCO or soldier with experience and potential. Infantry commanders are loath to lose their best men to the battalion's reconnaissance platoon (the traditional haven for the bright and fit infantry soldier) let alone to the SAS. The attitude of 'I've spent all this time training Private Jones and now someone else is going to reap the benefit while I have to train someone else to take his place' is all too common and understandable.

In the past, this view occasionally led to files being 'misfiled', letters 'lost' and messages 'mishandled'. The situation is reputed to be better now. A better understanding of the Regiment throughout the rest of the Army, together with a knowledge of the benefits that will be reaped when the SAS-trained soldier eventually returns,

Below: A four-man patrol takes a break during a 'tab' through South Wales. Two men rest while the other two keep watch.

have led to a better rapport between the Special Air Service and other units in the British Army. When endorsing and forwarding an application for SAS selection, the candidate's colonel can look forward to the not-too-distant future when the soldier comes back a highly trained and experienced leader who can pass on his hard-earned lessons to others.

It is not merely the strength of a volunteer's motivation that in question; it is important that the SAS ascertain that he is correctly motivated. The Regiment was faced with a problem in this area in the wake of the successful hostage-rescue mission at the Iranian embassy in London in May 1980. Interest, both civil and military, was aroused following the live TV broadcast of SAS Counter-Revolutionary Warfare (CRW) troops storming the besieged building. Suddenly, the Regiment went from being a little-known military formation to being a household name, and both the regular and the TA regiments became besieged by budding SAS 'operatives', all of them aspiring to be black-suited siege-busters.

'Suddenly everybody wanted to join, but for all the wrong reasons'

The fiasco that followed was not of the Regiment's making, as a former member of the 21st SAS Regiment's Training Wing explains:

'Of course, we were all pleased about the achievement of the Regulars at Princes Gate. What we weren't expecting was the sudden influx of prospective recruits to the Duke of York's [Barracks in Chelsea, which houses the headquarters of 21 SAS]. There were what appeared to be mile-long queues outside the office. Suddenly, everybody wanted to join, but for all the wrong reasons. Very few

Left: A freefall parachutist descending towards the clouds in a stable position at over 160km/h.
Below: A fully loaded SAS mobility troop Land Rover parked up in the desert. Desert vehicles, known as 'Pink Panthers', were painted pink to make them less visible to the enemy.

people understood what our role was, and most thought we spent most of our time abseiling down the sides of buildings. Some very strange types came in. We had prospective recruits coming in with concealed weapons — knives strapped around their ankles, the lot. I felt sorry for the usual TA soldiers who wanted to take selection and transfer across [to the SAS]. They had really chosen the wrong time to come along.'

'Very few who are unsuitable get through the system'

However, despite the sudden interest in the SAS, and the surge of volunteers — most of whom were totally unsuitable — the two TA SAS regiments managed to maintain their high standards. Well over 100 people attended the first cadre to be held after the Iranian embassy rescue, but only single figures passed through selection and went on to continuation training. One course actually had to be closed down because too many men dropped out. The regular SAS experienced similar problems, as a member of Training Wing points out:

'We had a lot of blokes volunteer, but for all the wrong reasons. Most dropped out because of the physical side. Some got through the early stages, but they obviously weren't suitable. If they didn't "jack it in", then they got "binned". Very few who are unsuitable get through the system, and those who do don't make it through continuation.'

The will to win against the odds is all important

Essentially then, the course is designed to be a test of the individual's mental as well as physical qualities, and it is conducted, under observation, in carefully controlled conditions. The series of 'beat-up' marches, which lead up to the final test, are intentionally hard, but graded to allow the candidates the best possible chance of success. After all, 22 SAS wants volunteers to pass the course, and while selection candidates are not actively encouraged, neither is there any longer any 'negative motivation'. This used to take the form of 'beasting', a practice whereby candidates were encouraged by 'well-meaning' instructors to take a short break, or even to give up completely — and 'RTU'd' (Returned To Unit), as they say in the SAS, if they succumbed. The will to win against the odds, and to overcome physical hardships through mental strength, is all important. Being neither encouraged nor cursed, a candidate's success depends solely on his own effort.

Much of the candidate's time during the early stages of selection is taken up with map-reading theory and practical land navigation. To many outsiders it may seem unusual that a soldier's map-reading skills may not be up to scratch, but many soldiers have only limited experience in this field, since, used to being led rather than leading, they are accustomed to relying on an NCO or officer to read the map and plot the course.

Practical map-reading is a vital SAS skill and it is tested to the full during selection. The Brecon Beacons, although undulating, lack the more obvious identifying features, such as buildings or roads. Also, visibility is often severely restricted, and students must become adept at marching on a compass bearing taken from a map rather than from a feature on the horizon.

At the start of selection the groups of candidates are divided up into pairs, but as the course progresses the men are deprived of the comfort of a partner and sent out on their own — and the stress levels rise. Each man sets off with a bergen, a map and a compass. He is given the grid reference of the first RV, and he must make it there in the best way that he can.

'You know it'll be like running up the side of a house — and it is'

Speed is important on these marches and there are time limits, but these are known only to the DS; nobody tells the candidate who is therefore unable to pace himself reliably. Neither is he told beforehand how many RVs there are, or where they are. All he knows for sure is where the next RV is, and only on reaching it does he find out where the one after that lies. This uncertainty serves to induce stress, which is further increased by special mental tests introduced by the DS.

For those few who make it through to Test Week, life only gets worse. By this time, the numbers on the course have thinned out considerably, giving the Directing Staff more time to concentrate on the individual. By now, the weight of the bergens will have increased from the original 11kg to 25kg, the maximum the men will carry during selection. Although fitter now than when they started, they are also very tired. Some will be completely exhausted, seemingly working on willpower alone.

The men and their abilities are constantly being observed and assessed. As they arrive at the various checkpoints SAS instructors evaluate their condition. Does this man have the ability to continue? Is he likely to become disorientated or collapse? If the answer is 'yes', the man is pulled off the course. Should this happen and

A trooper demonstrates abseiling technique during a mountain warfare exercise in North Wales. Rock-face skills have been essential to the SAS since World War II days.

the soldier has been doing the best he can, the Regiment may give him another chance on a later selection course. However, if a man 'jacks' — gives up — he is unlikely to get a second bite at the cherry.

The last hurdle for those who have got this far is a 60km march. Known as 'Long Drag', or the 'Fan Dance' — after Pen-Y-Fan, the highest peak in the Brecon Beacons — it is the last in the series of day and night land-navigation exercises that make up Test Week. Regardless of weather conditions, the volunteer — who by now will be wondering why he is doing all this — has to complete the course within a set period, usually 20 hours. The route for 'Long Drag' is chosen to encompass some of the highest peaks in the Brecons. As one SAS

First aid being applied to a 'sim cas' (simulated casualty) during an exercise. The men are wearing NBC kit without respirators.

man ruefully recalls, 'Now that mountain [Pen-Y-Fan] is a big, big bastard. You look up at it, and you know it'll be like running up the side of a house — and it is.'

To reach the final RV, almost any amount of pain is bearable

However, with the end now in sight, most men who start 'Long Drag' finish it. They have come too far to turn back now, and failure after all they have gone through is not an option to be considered. To reach the final RV in the time allotted, almost any amount of pain is bearable, for when 'Long Drag' is over, so is selection.

With selection successfully completed, the volunteers are past the first obstacle but are not yet in the SAS; they have three further phases of training to complete before they are 'badged'. The first of these is continuation training which teaches the soldiers basic SAS skills. Up to this

point, the men have been very much on their own. They began selection as strangers, coming as they did from different units of the British Army, and relationships between them have since been little more than nodding acquaintances. This is due to the nature of the training, with much of the candidate's time being spent on solo 'tabs' across the Beacons, and the rest in trying to grab some rest in between. Once on continuation training, however, the pace changes and the stress eases.

Although it is still possible to fail to gain entry into the Regiment at this stage, the course members now feel more confident. They have a shared experience, having been through selection and proved themselves capable of withstanding its rigours; they also have a common goal. The attitude of the SAS instructors has changed as well. They become more approachable and less of an apparent threat; the DS are still testing the men, but they are teaching them too.

There will be a marked difference in Standing Operating Procedures

Over the next 14 weeks, the prospective SAS troopers are involved in detailed, realistic training that is specifically designed to enable them to become part of a four-man patrol — the basic SAS operational unit. Operating as part of a four-man patrol is likely to be different from anything the men have done during their previous military service. The closest they will have come to it is if they have served in an infantry battalion's reconnaissance platoon, but even then there will be a marked difference in Standing Operating Procedures (SOPs).

During 'continuation', the potential SAS troopers are introduced to SAS SOPs, a term with which they will become increasingly familiar. Training is both theoretical and practical. Instruction is given in the basic skills vital to the SAS soldier: small patrol tactics, elementary signalling, first aid, demolitions, combat survival, jungle warfare and static-line parachuting.

Each man has his own specific role, and his own arc of fire

SAS patrol tactics differ from those used by other branches of the Army. In a four-man patrol, as opposed to an eight-man infantry section, each man has his own specific, individual role, and his own arc of fire, for which he is responsible while the patrol is on the move. The man in front, the lead scout, covers an arc of 180 degrees to the front. The man behind, usually the patrol commander, covers an arc to the left or the right, while the man behind him covers the area on the opposite side. The

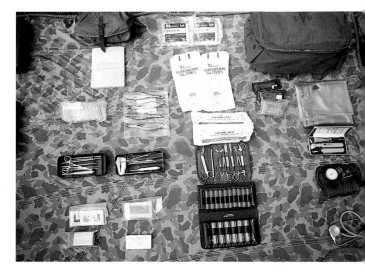

A special forces patrol medic's pack, showing the wide range of surgical and first aid items available to the SAS. Each four-man patrol has a medical specialist.

final man, or 'tail-end Charlie', is responsible for the arc to the rear of the patrol. In this way, the four-man patrol is able to move with maximum security. While undergoing continuation training, the members of a team are swapped about, each man getting the opportunity to take his place in a different position within the patrol, until all the men are conversant with the roles and responsibilities of each member of the team.

The four-man patrol is not designed to be an aggressive fighting unit

The four-man patrol is a close-knit group. First devised by Stirling when he formed the Regiment in the Western Desert, it has withstood the test of time and become the model for many of the world's special forces. It is small enough to move undetected, but large enough to put down sufficient fire to enable it to escape a contact. It is not designed to be an aggressive fighting unit, but rather to be self-sufficient. Should a fighting patrol or an ambush party be required for a particular operation, patrols are joined together, either into eight-man teams or complete troops of 16 men, depending on the tactical situation and the mission. Nevertheless the four-man patrol remains the basic operational unit, the cornerstone of the SAS, as its founder intended.

As the continuation course continues its tactical training, it is introduced to signalling. Communication is a skill vital to the SAS. Without the ability to maintain contact with their operational base, SAS patrols would be unable

to provide the higher authorities with the all-important information gleaned by their reconnaissance missions. Patrols would be unable to call in artillery and air strikes, or aircraft for exfiltration once a mission was completed. Over recent years, the ability to communicate has become increasingly important. Nowadays, all SAS soldiers must achieve Regimental Signaller standard, which involves, among other skills, transmitting and receiving morse code at a minimum of eight words per minute. In addition, all troopers must be conversant with the codes and ciphers used by the SAS.

Signalling within the SAS is a skill that must be mastered to a level of proficiency far greater than that required by communicators within infantry battalions, and indeed to a level higher than that of all but the most specialised operators within the Royal Corps of Signals, the British Army's communications experts. An indication of the professionalism required by the SAS in this field is illustrated by the number of different systems they have to operate. Most units employ a maximum of six different types of radio; the SAS use at least 30 different sets.

The soldiers learn about the handling and care of explosives

During the course of continuation training, potential SAS troopers are also introduced to first aid, SAS style. The medical skills taught by the Regiment are pitched at a number of levels. Initially instructed in basic first-aid techniques, such as how to resuscitate a casualty or how to stop bleeding, the troopers go on to learn about casualty-stabilisation and how to splint broken bones for medical evacuation. After getting to grips with the basics, the students learn more advanced techniques, such as how to set up an IV infusion (drip), how to administer drugs — both oral and injected — and the basics of casualty-handling and care.

In addition to signalling and first aid, basic demolitions techniques are also taught during continuation training. The soldiers learn about the handling and care of explosives, how to construct charges and, most importantly, where to place them. It is no use getting the explosives to the target, making up the charges, and then placing them where they do little or no damage. Prospective SAS troopers are instructed in identifying exactly the right spot to put the correct type of charge. An engineer explains:

'If you want to take out, say, a railway line, you probably wouldn't lay charges on the track itself. Blown tracks

A patrol signaller sends a message back to base, using continuous wave (CW), or morse code. Signals specialists are qualified to send and receive at eight words per minute.

are easy to repair — a couple of hours and you can lay new lines. So the only reason that you'd destroy the track itself would normally be if you wanted to derail a train. You'd find somewhere where the target, either the train or the railway line, passed through a tunnel or culvert, or across a bridge, then you'd blow the bridge, for instance. There is a picture taken of, I think, the Royal Marines in Korea. They are laying charges on a railway line, and in the background there is a tunnel. If they had taken out the tunnel, it would have caused maximum damage to the target. The photo serves as a good example of how not to do it.'

The trainees are dropped off in a remote part of the British Isles

After successfully negotiating this section of the continuation phase, the students move on to Combat and Survival Training, which lasts for about a week. During this part of the course, the prospective SAS troopers learn how to live off the land, how to evade capture, and, in case they do get caught, how to resist interrogation and how to escape.

Surviving in the wild is a skill which must be mastered by all. Initial theoretical instruction is given in the identification of food sources; the students are taught, for example, which plants are edible and where they can be found. The men learn how to build shelters using the materials to hand, how to lay snares to trap wild animals, and how to light fires using little more than their imagination. These skills are then tested when the trainees are dropped off in a remote part of the British Isles and left to fend for themselves. Wearing ancient battledress and old Army greatcoats, the men have to use the limited resources available to them to their best advantage. A group of three or four men might, if they are lucky, have a knife, a watch and a box of matches between them.

The men are blindfolded and led off to an interrogation centre

The Combat and Survival phase culminates in an Escape and Evasion (E&E) exercise in which the students are pursued by an 'enemy force' — which is usually a local infantry battalion, bent on proving themselves by capturing the trainee SAS men. The object for the trainees is of course to avoid capture, but even if they do, for the purposes of this exercise they suffer the same fate as those who are caught. Those still at large at the end of the exercise must make their way to a 'compromised' RV, where they will either be captured, or required to give themselves up within a certain period of time. Once captured,

the men are blindfolded, often with their hands tied behind their backs, and led off to an interrogation centre for the next stage in their training.— Resistance-To-Interrogation (RTI).

For many, the RTI phase is the worst part of their training so far, even worse than selection. It is an unnerving experience. A soldier who got this far describes how his RTI experience began:

The condition of those being interrogated is carefully monitored

'I was picked and led to a 'Rover where there was an SAS captain I knew quite well. I was blindfolded by him with one of my puttees — this was in the '70s, before the Boot (Combat, High). I was then placed face down in the back of the 'Rover with my hands tied behind my back. There were a couple of bodies underneath me, which was useful, as we were then driven off cross country and they absorbed most of the shock. There was quite a lot of swearing going on, but I didn't recognise the voices. Somewhere along the line to the holding centre, we were transferred to the back of a four-tonner. Getting into the back of a wagon with your hands tied behind your back and blindfolded is an interesting experience. The guards helped. I remember thinking at the time that I owed someone in the Royal Green Jackets [the regiment providing the search force] a couple of bruises.'

On arrival at the interrogation centre, each man is interviewed by a doctor, who gives him a once-over to check him for any physical problems, before being passed on to his interrogators. Each soldier signs a release form, but there is little actual physical abuse of the captives — and certainly no torture — during these RTI exercises, and the condition of those being interrogated is carefully monitored by experts.

For the captives RTI is 24 hours of purgatory

Exactly what happens during the interrogation phase cannot be discussed in great detail, but the aim, as one would expect, is to coerce the men into giving away information. A soldier is required to state only his name, rank, service number and date of birth. All other questions, regardless of their apparent insignificance, must be responded to with the phrase, 'I cannot answer that question.' Experienced interrogators rely on maintaining high levels of both physical and mental stress to break down their subjects' resistance. Despite the fact that treatment complies with the rules laid down in the Geneva accord, the situation of the captives is anything but comfortable.

For the 24 hours that the exercise lasts, the men on the course endure a gruelling series of interrogation sessions, between which they spend their time standing spreadeagled or squatting in various stress-inducing positions.

Getting through the RTI phase requires a great deal of self-control and commitment. Being constantly bombarded by questions and having to endure considerable discomfort when already exhausted does take its toll. The

On the grave markers:

BUD COOK
BUD WAS A
CHRONIC
FIRE-ARM WAVER
HE DIED QUITE
YOUNG
STILL A SHAVER

TODD
UNDER THIS SOD
LIES MORTIMER
TODD.
HE PUT HIS TRUST
IN A RUSTY ROD.

RIP
FRANK HOE
FOOLS MAY
COME
FOOLS MAY
GO
THIS ONE
WENT
HE WAS TO
SLOW

BILLY MISE
HE DIDN'T
PRACTISE
HERE HE
LIES

RIP
BILL DAY
FORGOT TO
LOAD
HERES HIS
PLOT

Above: A macabre reminder of "Don'ts" for those on selection and continuation training at Hereford.
Left: A trooper points out his position with a twig during a land navigation exercise. Map-reading skills are severely tested in selection.

most common reasons given for 'jacking it in' at this stage are 'I didn't see the point in going on' and 'If my own guys could do this to me, I didn't think it was worth finding out what the opposition might do.'

In fact, putting up with being interrogated 'by your own side' is, in many ways, more difficult than being questioned by the enemy, even should the latter use physical force. In continuation RTI, all the soldiers have to lose if they crack is a little pride and a place in the SAS; in an operational situation, there is a real need to keep silent, a real risk involved in imparting any information, however insignificant it may seem. The period of mock Tactical Questioning (TQ), as Resistance-To-Interrogation is known by the 'professional interrogators', is a severe

Above: A four-man patrol is briefed on its task by the intelligence officer. In the field, SAS maps are never marked, in case they fall into the wrong hands.

test conducted under conditions which are as realistic as possible. For the captives it is 24 hours of purgatory that reaffirms the individual's commitment to avoid capture at all costs.

Success during the RTI/TQ phase effectively marks the completion of continuation training and the prospective SAS soldiers' attention now turns to the Far East and the jungle warfare phase. Jungle operations have been an important part of 22 SAS' role since the unit's formation in Malaya and the Regiment takes this aspect of its work seriously. For the next four to six weeks the men will be on location in the exotic surroundings of, for example,

Right: A recruit 'tabbing' through South Wales during the final stages of selection. On his back is a bergen rucksack weighing around 25kg.

Above: Members of 23 SAS (V) are briefed before a weekend training exercise abroad.
Left: Escape and Evasion. Dressed in old-style battledress, a soldier lies low to avoid discovery by a patrol during a combat survival exercise.

Brunei, learning the ins-and-outs of what will be, for the majority of them, a totally unfamiliar environment.

After a period of acclimatisation, the students are given instruction in basic jungle survival skills. These include how to make use of the local flora and fauna for food — the trainees learn how to kill and cook a snake without being bitten or poisoned — and how to construct a jungle 'basha'. Students are also taught how to navigate and move in the restricted visibility of the jungle. Only when they are fully conversant with the skills, techniques and procedures necessary for successful operations in what is becoming for them a more familiar environment, are the men let loose in the jungle itself.

The students make eight descents, including one from a balloon

The jungle phase builds up to a demanding final exercise in which the candidates are divided into four-man patrols that have to successfully complete a series of realistic tasks. Once deployed, the patrols are on their own, and their only contact with the outside world is by radio. Should a real emergency occur, the patrol's only recourse is to their training, experience — and SOPs. There is no instructor with them to offer advice or assess their performance. The measure of success or failure in this final test of their ability is whether or not they achieve their objectives. Recently, one patrol became lost during the final exercise in the jungle phase. All four men were 'RTU'd'. A

The end of the game for one 'evadee' as he is 'collared' by infantrymen during a company sweep. In the end all candidates, caught or not, are taken in for interrogation.

severe penalty for failure at this late stage, but one demanded by the uncompromising standards of SAS.

Those who pass the jungle training phase are through the last major barrier between them and joining an SAS 'Sabre' squadron. All that now lies between them and their ultimate goal is the basic static-line parachute course. In fact some of the students, such as those from

The Parachute Regiment if there are any, may already be para-qualified and therefore over the finish line. The remainder face four weeks at No 1 Parachute Training School (PTS) at RAF Brize Norton in Oxfordshire.

All military parachute training is in the hands of the RAF and all Britain's airborne forces learn their parachuting at Brize Norton. Members of The Parachute Regiment and 5 Airborne Brigade, both TA soldiers and regulars, train alongside Royal Marine commandos; Navy personnel attached to the Marines work alongside RAF Regiment and RAF Parachute Jumping Instructors (PJIs) under training; and included in this all-arms, multi-forces mix in the PTS hangar are members of the SAS, usually small in number, doing exactly the same course as everyone else.

Over the four-week period, the students are introduced to the PX1 Mk4 and PX1 Mk5 main parachutes, and the PR7 reserve parachute. The Mk5 is only be used for the first jump, the Mk4 — commonly referred to as the PX4 — is used for the remainder. The PR7, hopefully, will not be used at all. The students make a total of eight descents, including one, the first jump, from a balloon, one at night and one operational descent.

The operational descent, the final jump on the course, was introduced by 5 Airborne Brigade in the mid-1980s. Instead of simply taking the soldiers up to 1000ft and despatching them from the aircraft, on this eighth descent the RAF add in certain extras. Once airborne and in clear airspace, the aircraft descends to around 350ft for a minimum of an hour of low-level flying. It may, for instance,

An eight-man patrol moves cross country during a winter warfare exercise in Norway. The SAS train all over the world; no-one knows where they may be called to serve next.

go up to Wales and fly along the valleys, which is good experience for the aircrew, but not for the less fortunate parachutists. An SAS trooper explains:

'I actually saw one PJI float off the ramp for a couple of seconds'

'The operational descent is a bit of a sickener, both in the classic and literal sense. It's designed to give you an idea of what an actual combat deployment by air would be like. As far as I know — and I've had experience of French, German and US systems — we are one of the only countries to do this. The Americans, for instance, jump from high-flying C-141s and usually exit the aircraft from 1200ft. Neither their aircraft, nor most of their crews, are capable of the type of flying required for an operational jump. It differs from normal training sorties and jumps in a number of ways. It entails servicing and stacking your bergens, which are containerised for parachuting, inside the aircraft before take-off. Normally, you carry them onto the aircraft with you and stow them between your legs...'

'So you're being thrown about in the back of the aircraft as it weaves its way down the valleys, probably the same ones you spent hours walking over during selection. You're hot and sticky, because the temperature is difficult to control after coming down from altitude. Anyway, that's the excuse the RAF gives out. Actually, conditions are pretty bad for them too, and I've seen RAF PJIs and "loadies" [loadmasters] throw up like the rest of us. I actually saw one PJI float off the ramp for a couple of seconds once, because the aircraft was pulling negative 'G' or something. Poor bastard went as green as his flight suit.'

There will be more people in the air and more chance of a collision

In addition to the discomfort of low-level flying, the men have other problems to occupy them. On an operational descent, the sticks — the number of men parachuting at one time — are larger than normal, with 14 or more jumpers on each side of the aircraft. This means that there will be more people in the air at one time immediately after the exit and therefore more chance of a collision. Also, the Dropping Zone (DZ) for this descent, although longer, is much rougher than the one at Weston-on-the-Green that they are used to, and the likelihood of injury is therefore greater.

A BV 202 over-snow vehicle leaves a bivvi-area during a snowstorm in Norway. Even exercises in these conditions barely prepared the SAS for South Georgia.

An SAS trooper prepares his parachute before a training jump with the Paras and Royal Marines. The SAS follow the same basic para course as the rest of the Armed Forces.

Around P-Hour minus 40 — that is, 40 minutes before the jump is due to take place — the bergens are handed down and hooked onto the parachute harnesses. It is difficult to do this in the cramped, confined conditions, but the RAF PJIs are excellent instructors and the drills are simple and easy to remember. Checks are then carried out on equipment, the parachutists hook up their static lines to the overhead cable, and the side doors are opened. By this time, it's approximately 'P' minus five.

The men return to Hereford, where they are 'badged' SAS

The parachutists are now lined up along the sides of the aircraft and the PJIs take their positions at the doors. After what seems like an eternity of discomfort and anticipation the green light goes on and the first parachutists, one on each side of the aircraft, exit from 800ft. They are followed in quick succession by the next pair and the next, while inside the plane their colleagues, their heavy containers held before them, shuffle towards the door and freedom. Within moments the whole course is out of the aircraft and enjoying that great feeling of relief which is rivalled only by that felt on a safe landing — one you walk away from. No one likes an operational descent.

This final jump marks the end of the SAS trooper's training. The following day there is dekitting and the course debrief in the morning, and the 'wings' parade in the afternoon. The SAS contingent are awarded their 'Sabre' wings, while the remainder of the course receive the normal parachute wings, worn by all Britain's airborne forces and para-qualified commando forces. The style of 'wings' awarded does not reflect any difference in parachute training, rather it reflects differences in the training the men have undergone before arriving at PTS.

On completion of the 'wings' course at Brize Norton, the men return to Hereford, where they are 'badged' SAS and join one of the Regiment's four 'Sabre', or fighting, squadrons. Each of these is divided into four troops of 16 men, and each troop is divided in turn into four patrols of four men each. Additionally each troop within a squadron is has its own specialised role: Boat Troop — amphibious warfare; Mobility Troop — Land Rovers and motorcycles; Air Troop — freefall parachuting; and Mountain Troop — mountain and winter warfare.

On assignment to one of these troops the new-arrival starts training in the particular specialisation. The trooper in Boat Troop, for instance, will learn combat swimming and the handling techniques of small assault craft and two-man canoes; in Air Troop he will be taught Military Free Fall (MFF) parachuting; in Mobility Troop he will learn how to drive and maintain Land Rovers and other vehicles; and in Mountain Troop he will be instructed in special climbing skills and high-altitude movement.

25 or even 50 per cent casualties is an ever-present threat

The newly badged SAS soldier serves a probationary period of 12 months which starts from the date on which he was first selected for training. During this phase, in addition to beginning to learn the role of the troop to which he is assigned, the SAS trooper learns a personal, or patrol, skill. In a four-man patrol each member has one primary speciality — medicine, demolitions, communications or languages — with the result that each of the four specialities deemed necessary for successful SAS operations is represented at a high standard within each patrol. As the trooper spends more time with the Regiment, he will pick up a second, or even a third, patrol skill. Cross-training is vital in a unit that operates in four-man patrols, where 25 or even 50 per cent casualties as result of a contact with the enemy is an ever-present threat. Were troopers not trained in other specialisations, such losses would automatically doom a mission to failure.

Specialist skills enhance a patrol's ability to operate independently

At the end of the probationary year, SAS soldiers take their place as fully fledged members of a four-man patrol within their particular troop and go on to advanced training in the SAS disciplines mentioned. Those who display an aptitude for languages may be sent to the Army School of Languages at Beaconsfield, where popular courses include German and Russian. Learning a language properly takes time and the advanced Russian language course alone lasts 18 months. Advanced courses for medics are shorter, but no less interesting. All SAS soldiers receive some medical training, but some troopers opt to further their skills. These men are assigned to selected hospitals in the UK, where they work and train in casualty rooms and operating theatres. It should be pointed out that training at all levels and in all skills is a continuous process for the SAS trooper — a fully trained SAS soldier does not exist. Specialist skills such as medicine and foreign languages enhance a patrol's ability to operate independently, but troop skills are no less important: reaching a target can often depend on the use of more than one troop skill, just as the ultimate success of a patrol may depend on an SAS soldier having more than one individual skill. For instance, should an operation call for a freefall parachute drop into a mountainous area, the obvious personnel to conduct it would be those with experience with both a Mountain Troop and an Air Troop. The SAS training system endeavours to ensure that these people exist.

The Regiment lives up to the motto 'Train hard, Fight easy'

The standard tour of duty with the SAS, for both officers and men, is three years. At the end of this period, non-commissioned ranks may opt for a further three years; officers must return to their units at tour-end. This is not as unfair as it may appear. Quite simply, officers' promotion requirements are different to those of NCOs and soldiers. Officer promotion depends on experience in a number of fields, and 22 SAS is limited in what it can offer

in this respect. However, officers are not barred from the Regiment after one tour; indeed a number who serve with the SAS as troop commanders return later as squadron commanders, and may even come back again in a more senior post.

The SAS training schedule is punishing and unrelenting; it has to be if the Regiment is to remain capable of fulfilling the variety of tasks to which it is committed. From selection through continuation, jungle training and the 'wings' course, there is no let-up. And it does not end there. Once qualified, the members of the SAS can expect to spend around six to eight months away from Hereford every year; about half of this time will be spent overseas, usually on a squadron detachment. The Regiment lives up to the motto 'Train hard, Fight easy'.

Below: A soldier attached to the SAS looks on as a patrol prepares to jump from the ramp of a C-130. This technique is not taught on basic para, where exits are from the side door.

Above: SAS troops boarding a C-130 Hercules at a US air base during a NATO exercise. The Regiment is constantly training, a fully trained SAS soldier does not exist.

Yet the SAS is not for everybody. Many volunteer; few are selected. This does not reflect on their competence as soldiers. The SAS is different to other branches of the Army. It specialises in small-unit operations where great emphasis is necessarily placed on the individual. This is in contrast to most other units, where soldiers work in larger groups in which teamwork is important and individual responsibility is less heavy at the lower levels. To join the SAS requires enormous self-confidence and motivation plus fitness, determination and outstanding military proficiency. But for those cut out for it, there is no doubt that the Regiment offers the ultimate in soldiering.

SPECIAL FORCES ON TRIAL

The Special Air Service Regiment is a universally respected special operations force with a history of excellence going back to the Malayan Emergency and beyond to World War II; it is also an experienced and effective counter-terrorist unit with a proven track record. Today many countries — both in the East and in the West — have similar units. Who, are these forces, how do they compare with the SAS and what do they have in common with the Special Air Service?

The SAS have close links with many units around the world. These ties may be historical, as they are with certain French and Belgian units which fought in the British SAS Brigade during World War II, and which still wear SAS badges and insignia as part of their uniforms. Or they may be working relationships with special forces of other nations, whether they be multi-role military organisations, such as US Army Special Forces, or specifically tasked units, like GSG-9 and GIGN — the West German and French counter-terrorist groups respectively.

Special forces are inclined to be similar in many respects. Their activities are generally cloaked in secrecy and the very nature of their work dictates that they must be teams of highly trained specialists. In addition, in much the same way as airborne troops world wide, special operations forces tend to share a common bond. Nevertheless differences do exist — in size, in structure, in training, in methods and in role. A comparison of some of the major organisations shows just where the SAS fits into the world of special forces, and how its

US Navy SEALs, armed with US and West German weapons, come ashore.